WRITERS AT WORK

A Guide to Basic Writing

WRITERS AT WORK

A Guide to Basic Writing

Jill Singleton
Towson University

St. Martin's Press
New York

Editorial Director, ESL/ELT: *Tina B. Carver*
Associate Editor: *Kimberly Wurtzel*
Manager, Publishing Services: *Emily Berleth*
Assistant Editor, Publishing Services: *Meryl Gross*
Project Management: *Tünde A. Dewey/Dewey Publishing Services*
Production Supervisor: *Scott Lavelle*
Text Design: *Wee Design Group*
Graphics: *Anna DiVito*
Photo Research: *Inge King*
Cover Design: *Evelyn Horowicz*

Library of Congress Catalog Card Number: 97-065182

Manufactured in the United States of America.

3 2 1 0 9 8
f e d c b a

For information, write:
St. Martin's Press
175 Fifth Avenue
New York, NY 10010

ISBN: 0-312-13731-1

to Phil, of course

Contents

PREFACE   xi

BEGIN AT THE BEGINNING   1
    (Introduction to the Writing Process)

CHAPTER 1   A MORNING PERSON OR A NIGHT PERSON?   9
    Get Ideas   11
      (Brainstorming)
    Organize Your ideas   11
      (Choosing and Adding)
    Write   11
      (First Draft)
    Revise   11
      (Relevance)
    Edit   15
      (The Simple Sentence)
    A Step Further: An Advertisement   22

CHAPTER 2   A PERSON IMPORTANT TO YOU   23
    Get Ideas   25
      (Brainstorming)
    Organize Your Ideas   25
      (By Category)
    Write   27
      (First Draft)
    Revise   28
      (Topic and Supporting Sentences)
    Edit   33
      (Fragments and Run-Ons)
    A Step Further: A Collage   40

CHAPTER 3 THE WEEKEND!   41

Get Ideas   43
  (Webbing)
Organize Your Ideas   44
  (By Number)
Write   44
  (First Draft)
Revise   44
  (Transitions of Time)
Edit   47
  (The Compound Sentence)
A Step Further: The Perfect Weekend   53

CHAPTER 4 A SCARY OR FUNNY EXPERIENCE   55

Get Ideas   57
  (Sharing Stories)
Organize Your Ideas   57
  (Interview)
Write   58
  (First Draft)
Revise   58
  (Adding Details)
Edit   62
  (Compound Sentence Run-Ons)
A Step Further: A Radio Program   67

CHAPTER 5 HOLIDAYS   69

Get Ideas   71
  (Webbing)
Organize Your Ideas   71
  (Making a Chart/Sharing)
Write   72
  (First Draft)
Revise   72
  (Conclusions)
Edit   76
  (Complex Sentences)
A Step Further: A Holiday Party!   83

CHAPTER 6   UNFINISHED STORIES   85

Get Ideas   88
(Group Discussion)

Organize Your Ideas   88
(Time Order)

Write   88
(First Draft)

Revise   89
(Group Reading)

Edit   90
(Complex Sentence Fragments)

A Step Further: A Play   94

CHAPTER 7   A FAVORITE PLACE   95

Get Ideas   97
(Drawing)

Organize Your Ideas   98
(By Space)

Write   100
(First Draft)

Revise   100
(Drawing Your Partner's Place)

Edit   102
(Prepositions of Place)

A Step Further: A Tourist Brochure   106

CHAPTER 8   THE IDEAL SPOUSE   107

Get Ideas   109
(Freewriting)

Organize Your Ideas   110
(By Importance)

Write   112
(First Draft)

Revise   112
(Transitions of Enumeration)

Edit   115
(Sentence Variety)

A Step Further: A Pen Pal   119

CHAPTER 9   WHAT'S YOUR OPINION?   121

Get Ideas   122
(Discussing and Freewriting)
Organize Your Ideas   122
(Outlining)
Write   128
(First Draft)
Revise   128
(Outlining Your Partner's Paper)
Edit   130
(Class Checklist)
A Step Further: Letters to the Editor   131

CHAPTER 10   TEN YEARS FROM NOW   133

Get Ideas   135
(Student Choice)
Organize Your Ideas   135
(By Category)
Write   135
(First Draft)
Revise   135
(Student Checklist)
Edit   136
(Student Checklist)
A Step Further: A Day in the Life of . . .   136

QUICK CHECK: AN EDITING GUIDE TO ACADEMIC ENGLISH

Marking Symbols   137
How to Use *Quick Check*   138

V—Verb Problem   139
Some Irregular Verbs   142
Other Verb Problems   143

S/V—Subject/Verb Agreement   144

Frag—Sentence Fragment   145

RO—Run-on Sentence   146

WF—Word Form   148

WW—Wrong Word   151

SP—Spelling   155

P—Punctuation   158

C—Capitalization   160

Preface

Writers at Work is a high-beginning/low-intermediate text aimed at preparing non-native speakers of English to write academic English. Its main goal is to put students on the path to becoming independent writers, confident in their growing ability to write in English. This focus arose from the frustrations that I felt as a student writer and that my students have shared with me over the years.

In high school and college, my teachers gave me plenty of *what* to write but never taught me *how* to write it. I remember long periods spent gazing at a blank page, waiting for inspiration. I never knew that "inspiration" was something that I could have control over. In classroom discussions and conferences, my students have reported writing experiences similar to mine. That is why I believe all students, particularly those with little experience of writing in English, need to be overtly taught and then guided in using the process of writing, which is, after all, nothing more than the steps which experienced writers have always followed when they write. With the ability to use the writing process, students have the knowledge and confidence they need to tackle further writing tasks in their academic careers.

Some teachers have been concerned that focusing on the process of writing leads to neglect of the final product. I believe that the opposite is true. Rightly understood, the writing process encompasses both creativity and careful refining. The final product is all the better for the writer's having spent sufficient time prewriting, drafting, and redrafting. *Writers at Work* attempts to guide students through the writing process in such a way that their final pieces of writing are both expressive and clear.

STRUCTURE AND CONTENT

- ∎ The book begins with an introductory section, "Begin at the Beginning," which teaches the writing process, including its recursive nature.

- ∎ Ten chapters follow, focusing on paragraph writing for the first eight chapters and moving on to simple multi-paragraph writing for the last two. Each chapter is composed of five parts, following the process of writing: (1) get ideas, (2) organize ideas, (3) write, (4) revise, and (5) edit. Strategies and skills are taught cumulatively through the chapters.

- Students start composing their own pieces of writing at the very beginning of each chapter, and all instruction is immediately applied to their own writing.

- Chapters are thematic, and all of the activities and exercises in the chapter relate to the theme. In this way, students can discover vocabulary to use in their own writing on the theme.

- Student interaction is important in *Writers at Work*. Throughout the book, students are carefully guided to help each other write more clearly and think more critically about writing.

- Systematic and cumulative instruction in paragraph construction and in building sentences in academic English is presented in a logical and manageable way. A major goal of *Writers at Work* is to help students, bit by bit, to revise and edit their own writing.

- At the end of each chapter is a section called "A Step Further . . . ." This section gives an optional activity through which students can share their writing with one another and explore the topic further by writing in a different genre or using a different skill. This section is also intended for fun!

- "Quick Check," an editing reference, closes the book. It is a mini-grammar reference dealing with the most common basic writing errors. It can be used by students when editing their writing or by teachers as extra help for an individual student. Instruction is provided for the students in "How to Use Quick Check," which is arranged according to a set of marking symbols.

SUPPLEMENTAL WRITING

No writing text can encompass the activity of an entire writing class. It is essential that students do a lot of unstructured writing in addition to the text's more structured writing in order to increase their fluency and comfort in writing in English. Activities such as journals, dialogue journals, informal letter-writing, and impromptu skits are vital to the growth of the students' writing ability. It is highly recommended that the teacher include such activities in the class.

FINAL NOTE

In the past it was often thought that students at lower writing levels were not capable of much beyond controlled composition. Over the years, however, I have found that even beginners, with encouragement and help, can express—and prefer to express—their own thoughts and ideas in their writing. It is a very satisfying experience to help students begin to find their own voices in English.

Acknowledgments

Writing a book is an arduous task, and I never would have completed it without the help and support of a lot of people. In fact, I never would have begun it without the encouragement of Nancy Pfingstag, who, as a consultant at United Arab Emirates University, first suggested that I try my hand at writing a textbook. Thank you, Nancy. I would also like to thank all of my students at the English Language Center of Towson University for their generosity in sharing their writing and insights. I am very grateful, too, to all of my fellow teachers and the staff at the ELC for giving me the support and chocolate I needed to complete this book, especially Katie Kauffman, an unselfish fount of ideas, Christine Kay Williams, my "shepherd" through the book-writing process, and Alice Gilbert, my old buddy.

I would like to thank the following reviewers for St. Martin's Press for their comments and suggestions: Charlotte Gilman, Texas Intensive English Program; Judith T. Matsunobu, Atlantic Community College; Mary Ann O'Brien, Interlink Language Center; Mary Ellen Ryder, Boise State University; May Shin, San Francisco State University; Kathryn Wada, Cypress College; and Barbara Yanez, Mt. San Antonio Community College.

Finally, thank you to my husband, Philip Singleton, for all your sacrifices that made it possible for me to write this book.

Many thanks to the following students for allowing me to use their writing:

Sami Al-Wehaibi
Osama Bulbul
Maria Coronado
Jeeyeon Jang
Hyung Kyu Kang
Hee Seung Lee
Shan Yih Liu
Aymeric Menargues
Myung Hwan Moon
Jin Seok Park
Jeongin Pu
Diana Rangel
Jung Youn Sim
Meltem Sisman
In-Hyuk Song
Nuraputra Sudrajat
Yoji Yamada
Shu-Hui Yang

WRITERS AT WORK

A Guide to Basic Writing

Begin at the Beginning

You are a writer. You are a writer in your own language, and soon you will be a writer in English. In your native language, you are probably a good writer. Think about writing in your own language. When you must write something for a class in your country, what do you do? Do you begin to write immediately, or do you think about your ideas first? After you write it, do you change anything? Do you write it one time or several times?

When writers with experience write, they follow the *process of writing*. A process is the steps to do something. First, you do one thing. Next, you do another thing, and then you do something else. The writing process is the steps experienced writers everywhere use when they write.

To understand the idea of a *process,* we will look at something in everyday life that follows a process.

A classmate invited Jenny to a party on Saturday night. It is now Saturday evening. Jenny is getting ready to go to the party. Put the steps in the process of getting ready in order.

THE PROCESS OF GETTING READY TO GO OUT

A. get dressed   **B.** get clothes ready   **C.** choose clothes   **D.** take a bath   **E.** fix hair

1. _____   2. _____   3. _____   4. _____   5. _____

Writing also follows a process. There are some steps that experienced writers usually follow. Put the steps of the *process of writing* in order.

THE PROCESS OF WRITING

A. organize ideas   **B.** revise (check ideas)   **C.** write   **D.** edit (check grammar)   **E.** get ideas

1. _____   2. _____   3. _____   4. _____   5. _____

These are the steps in the writing process. Every time you write a paragraph for this class, you should follow this process. All of the chapters in this book follow the process of writing, so it will be easy for you to practice using the process.

Should you use these steps *every* time you write something? No. Many kinds of writing do not need the process. For example, when you write a letter to a friend, write down a telephone message, or take notes in class, you do not use the writing process. But in this book, you are learning to write for your classes. It is a good idea to follow the steps in writing when you write for class. Why? Talk about that with your class.

Are you ready to begin?

WAIT A MINUTE!
THAT ISN'T REAL LIFE.

HERE'S THE WAY I REALLY GET READY TO GO OUT.

WHAT ABOUT ME?
THAT ISN'T THE WAY
I WRITE, EITHER.

THIS IS HOW EXPERIENCED
WRITERS REALLY WRITE.

He's right!

Life is messy. Life doesn't happen step by step. Writing is the same. Experienced writers move forward and backward among the steps. For example, while you are writing your paragraph (Step 3), you may think of a better way to organize your ideas (Step 2). While you are revising your paragraph (Step 4), you may think of some new ideas to add (Step 1). That's good! That is how experienced writers really write. You can improve your writing if you do the same.

CHAPTER **1**

A Morning Person or a Night Person?

Do you like the morning or the night better? Do you like to wake up early in the morning, or stay up late at night? Are you a morning person or a night person?

In this chapter, you will write about the time of day that you like the best. You can tell why you like the morning or the night and what you do in the morning or at night.

1. _____

_____

_____

2. _____

_____

_____

3. _____

_____

_____

1. _____

_____

_____

2. _____

_____

_____

3. _____

_____

_____

Talk about each photograph. Then write your answers to the questions.

1. What is happening in the photograph?
2. How do the people in the photograph feel?
3. Do you like to do the activity in the photograph?

GET IDEAS

One way to get ideas for your paragraph is to *brainstorm*. Brainstorming means to make a list of ideas. First, write the main idea at the top of the paper. Then try to write down all of your ideas about the main idea. Try to write down a lot of ideas. Some will be good ones. Others won't be useful for this paragraph. But list *all* the ideas that you can think of. Later you can choose the ideas that you want to use for your paragraph. When you brainstorm, the important thing is to write down as many ideas as possible.

As a class, brainstorm the words *morning* and *night*. Write down all of your ideas in a class list. Remember to use the words from the photo page.

ORGANIZE YOUR IDEAS

A. Choose to write about either the morning or the night.

B. Look at the class list of words for either morning or night. Copy onto your paper all of the words from the class list that you want to use.

C. Add any more words that are important for your paragraph. Be sure that you have words to tell *why you like* the morning or the night and *what you do* in the morning or at night.

WRITE

It is time to write your paragraph the first time. Get comfortable and relax!

Write your paragraph about the morning or the night. Be sure to write about *why you like* the morning or the night and *what you do* then.

Remember, after you write your paragraph, you will check it two times (revise and edit). You will have plenty of time to make it better. Now try to write your ideas in an interesting way, and don't worry about making mistakes.

REVISE

A. After you write your paragraph, you need to revise it. Remember that *revise* means to check your _____.

Read this student's paragraph about the night. What do you like about this paragraph? How could it be better?

> ### Night
>
> Night is the best time for me. In the evening. I call my friends. We go to a dance club. And have a happy time. My brother doesn't like to come with us. He stays home and studies. My friends and I dance and talk to our girlfriends or other people. Later, go to a coffee shop. We talk for a long time while we drink coffee and smoke. My brother thinks I should not smoke. He says I will kill myself with cigarettes. Then we each go to our own home. At home, I drink one more cup of coffee. And listen to the music of silence. I look out the window. How beautiful is the moon! Some men have walked on it. I look at the moon. Think about my future. The clock says midnight. Everything silent, serene, and perfect. I feel like midnight, too.

This paragraph has many good ideas in it. But it also has some ideas that do not belong in it. **In English, each paragraph should be about only one main idea.** All of the sentences in the paragraph should talk about the main idea. If a sentence talks about the main idea, it is a *relevant* sentence. Relevant means *related to* or *about* the main idea. If a sentence does not talk about the main idea, the sentence is *irrelevant* (not relevant). You should always take irrelevant sentences out of your paragraph.

Exercise 1

Cross out the irrelevant word in each group.

MORNING	AFTERNOON	EVENING	NIGHT
breakfast	lunch	dinner	sunshine
dance club	work	watch the news	do homework
read the paper	classes	wash dishes	relax
new day	moon	sunrise	call family

Exercise 2

In each group of sentences, one of the sentences is irrelevant. Write an ✘ next to the irrelevant sentence. Why is it irrelevant?

A.

_____ 1. It is quiet and peaceful early in the morning.

_____ 2. I like the fresh feeling in the air.

_____ 3. I go jogging then because there are few cars on the roads.

_____ 4. Some people are tired and cranky in the morning.

B.

_____ 1. My cat loves the night, of course.

_____ 2. He goes hunting for mice then.

_____ 3. Dead mice make me sick.

_____ 4. He also fights with other cats at night.

C.

_____ 1. My sister can't keep her eyes open after ten at night.

_____ 2. I think the best time of the day is after midnight.

_____ 3. I love to stay up and watch old movies on TV.

_____ 4. It is also a good time to read and listen to music.

Exercise 3

1. Reread the student's paragraph about the night. What is the main idea of the paragraph?
2. Are all of the sentences relevant to the main idea? If you see any irrelevant sentences, draw a line (———) through them.

Remember, do not worry about grammar mistakes now. You will correct the grammar later. Now look only at the ideas.

Exercise 4

Read the following student's paragraph about the morning. Think about the main idea. If you see any irrelevant sentences, draw a line (———) through them.

In the Morning

I love the early morning! I listen to the songs of the birds. The sun's rays enter my room. Through the window. Every night, I sit by the window and look for the moon. I always leave the curtains open for the morning sun. I always walk. In the early morning. My husband is still asleep. He hates the morning. I energetic and peaceful. My day starts happy. Then, I cook my breakfast. And take a shower. I begin to study. Also listen to music because I feel happy. In the morning. Time passes very fast. I think the morning is more productive than the night.

B. Now you are ready to revise your paragraph. It is a good idea to get help from a classmate. Another reader can help you to see your own paragraph more clearly. You can help another student also. Think about the best way to help your classmate. You should be both honest and careful.

1. Exchange your paper with another student. Read your partner's paragraph. What do you like about it? Put a star (★) next to any word, sentence, or idea that you like.

2. Do all of the sentences talk about the main idea? Does the paragraph have any irrelevant sentences? If you think a sentence is irrelevant, put parentheses ( ) around it.

3. Get your paper back from your partner. Reread your own paragraph. Did your partner find any irrelevant sentences? Do you agree that the sentences are irrelevant? If you agree, put a line through the irrelevant sentences. Also, look for any other irrelevant sentences that your partner did not find.

Rewrite your paragraph and make any changes that you need to.

Before you edit, talk about the following idea with your class.

In your mind, think about this picture. After high school, you go away to a university. Your good friend stays home. When you return home on vacation, you visit your friend. Of course, you are very happy to see each other. How do you greet your friend? Do you hug, kiss, or slap your friend on the back? Do you shake hands or bow? What do you say?

Then you visit your favorite teacher at your high school. You are also happy to see him or her. How do you greet your teacher? Do you greet the teacher in the same way as your friend? Do you hug, kiss, or slap your teacher on the back? Do you shake hands or bow? What do you say? Do you say the same thing that you say to your friend?

You probably do not greet your friend and your teacher in the same way. Is it wrong to speak one way to your friend and a different way to your teacher? No. Your friend and your teacher would be surprised if you greeted them in the same way. We all learn to use *appropriate* language. Appropriate means right for that person, time, or place. The opposite of appropriate is *inappropriate*. Appropriate language for your friend is sometimes inappropriate language for your teacher. Appropriate language for your teacher is sometimes inappropriate language for your friend.

The same is true in writing. In this book, you are learning to write for school. School writing is called *academic writing*. Appropriate language for academic writing is sometimes different than appropriate language for other kinds of writing. For example, your friend would be surprised if you wrote him or her a letter using academic language. We use different kinds of language for different kinds of writing. In school, you will need to use language appropriate for academic writing, so that is the language you will learn about in this book.

EDIT

A. After you are satisfied with the ideas in your paragraph, you are ready to edit it. Remember that *edit* means to check the _____.

Look at the paragraph about the night earlier in this chapter(page 12). Some of the sentences make the paragraph difficult to read. We will now look at how to make a sentence in academic English.

Exercise 1

Look at these sentences. Decide if they are appropriate or inappropriate for academic English. Write *A* (for appropriate) or *I* (for inappropriate) next to each sentence.

_____ 1. Night is the best time for me.

_____ 2. In the evening.

_____ 3. I call my friends.

_____ 4. We go to a dance club.

_____ 5. And have a happy time.

_____ 6. Everything silent, serene, and perfect.

Compare your answers with your classmates' answers. Later in this chapter, you will come back to this exercise and check your answers again.

What is a subject? A *subject* tells *who* or *what* the sentence is about.

1. Jackie hates the morning.

2. She never gets up or speaks to anyone before nine o'clock.

3. Every morning, her mother and father wake up at six o'clock.

4. They can't understand Jackie.

What is a verb? A *verb* tells what the subject *is* or *does*.

1. Jackie hates the morning.

2. She never gets up or speaks to anyone before nine o'clock.

3. Every morning, her mother and father wake up at six o'clock.

4. They can't understand Jackie.

Exercise 2

Decide if these words are subjects or verbs. Make a list of subjects and a list of verbs.

I	aunt and uncle	like	eats	night	roommate
am	newspaper	snore	she	is	thinks

_____ _____

_____ _____

_____ _____

_____ _____

_____ _____

_____ _____

Exercise 3

Find and underline the subjects and verbs in these sentences. Write *S* for subject and *V* for verb. The first one has been done for you.

    S V

1. <u>Dave likes</u> afternoons the best.

2. He gets up early in the morning for his classes.

3. His eyes often close in his 8:00 A.M. class.

4. At 12:30, he meets his friends and eats lunch with them.

5. Dave and his friends play soccer in the afternoon.

6. Soccer is their favorite sport.

7. After soccer, everyone has something to drink together.

8. Then Dave eats dinner and starts to study.

Now look back at Exercise 1 on page 13. Do you agree with your first answers?

Something to Remember

In English, the **subject** usually comes before the **verb** in the sentence.

Exercise 4

Put these words in the right order to make sentences. Sometimes there are several right answers. You only need to write one right answer. Remember to begin each sentence with a capital letter and to put a period at the end of each sentence.

Example: at / get up / 7:30 / I

<u>I get up at 7:30.</u>   OR   <u>At 7:30, I get up.</u>

1. the cafeteria / I / for / to / breakfast / go

   _____

2. morning / I / in / the / go / classes / to

   _____

3. order / at / pizza / my / roommate / noon / I / and

   _____

4. I / bed / in / on / study / afternoon / the / my / usually

   _____

5. in / the / my / visit / me / evening / friends

   _____

6. we / and / music / stereo / talk / play / on / my

   _____

7. from / to / 11:30 / read / I / 12:00 / midnight

   _____

8. light / turn / out / I / at / midnight / my

   _____

Exercise 5

The paragraph on the next page has no punctuation or capital letters. Decide where the sentences begin and end. Put a capital letter at the beginning of each sentence and a period or a question mark at the end. All of the sentences are simple sentences. The first sentence has been done for you.

Daylight Savings Time

In the United States, we have daylight savings time in the summer. *I* In late spring, we put

our clocks forward one hour then we have an extra hour of daylight every day

farmers are happy for the extra hour to work in the fields children have more time to play

outside their parents are happy about that adults have time to play on softball teams

after work everyone likes the extra sun in the summer

Exercise 6

As a class, look at this paragraph. Decide which sentences use appropriate language and which do not. Change the inappropriate language and write your answer in the space below the sentences. Notice that the writer took out all the irrelevant sentences.

Night

(1) Night is the best time for me. (2) In the evening. (3) I call my

_____

friends. (4) We go to a dance club. (5) And have a happy time. (6) My

_____

friends and I dance and talk to our girlfriends or other people. (7) Later,

_____

go to a coffee shop. (8) We talk for a long time while we drink coffee

_____

and smoke. (9) Then we each go to our own home. (10) At home, I drink

_____

one more cup of coffee. (11) And listen to the music of silence. (12) I look

_____

out the window. (13) How beautiful is the moon! (14) I look at the

_____

moon. (15) Think about my future. (16) The clock says midnight.

_____

(17) Everything silent, serene, and perfect. (18) I feel like midnight, too.

_____

Exercise 7

Look at this paragraph again. Decide which sentences use appropriate language and which do not. Change the sentences with the inappropriate language. Notice that the writer took out all the irrelevant sentences.

In the Morning

(1) I love the early morning! (2) I listen to the songs of the birds.

_____

(3) The sun's rays enter my room. (4) Through the window. (5) I always

_____

leave the curtains open for the morning sun. (6) I usually walk. (7) In

_____

the early morning. (8) I energetic and peaceful. (9) My day starts

_____

happy. (10) Then, I cook my breakfast. (11) And take a shower. (12) I

_____

begin to study. (13) Also listen to music because I feel happy. (14) In

_____

the morning. (15) Time passes very fast. (16) I think the morning is

_____

more productive than the night.

_____

B. Now, look at your own paragraph about the morning or the night. Look at each sentence. <u>Underline</u> all the subjects and circle all the verbs. Does every sentence have both a subject and a verb? If not, try to fix them.

Rewrite your paragraph in academic form. Academic form is shown on the next page.

Looking Good

This is the way an academic English paper looks. You should use large paper with a line on the left side. First, write your name in the upper right corner of the page. You should write the date under it. Then, put the title in the middle of the first line. You should not write on the second line.

Begin the paragraph on the third line. Remember to indent the first word of the paragraph. (You can see an example of an indent at the very beginning of this paragraph.) All other lines should begin at the left margin line. Also, don't write on every line. Write on every other line. You should write as neatly as you can. If you do all of these things, it will be easy to read and enjoy your writing.

An Advertisement

A. Many night people hate the morning. Many morning people like to go to bed early. Your job is to make an advertisement "selling" your favorite time of day. If you are a morning person, you will make an advertisement to get night people to enjoy the morning. If you are a night person, you will make an advertisement to get morning people to stay awake and enjoy the night.

B. Everyone in the class should bring in some advertisements from magazines, newspapers, junk mail, etc. Look at the ads. How do they sell things? Get some ideas from the advertisements.

C. Imagine that your advertisement will be in a magazine. Take a piece of paper the right size for a magazine. Make your advertisement. You can draw it, design it on a computer, make it by cutting out words and pictures from magazines— anything you like! Remember, your job is to "sell" people your favorite time of day. You want them to enjoy your favorite time of day.

D. Put all the class paragraphs and advertisements in a class magazine. Keep the magazine in a place where everyone can look at it.

CHAPTER 2

A Person Important to You

No man is an island. A famous English writer wrote this line. What do you think it means?

Everyone needs other people. Think about the important people in your life. Whom do you love, trust, and admire? Is it your father, mother, grandfather, grandmother, sister, brother, or cousin? Is it a friend, boyfriend or girlfriend, husband or wife, teacher, or someone else? Why are they important to you?

Picture This...

1. _____

_____

_____

_____

_____

2. _____

_____

_____

_____

_____

_____

1. _____

_____

_____

_____

_____

2. _____

_____

_____

_____

_____

Talk about each photograph. Then write your answers to the questions.

1. Who is the person in the photograph? Write your ideas.
2. How can you describe the person?

GET IDEAS

Now you will get ideas about a person important to *you*.

A. Make a list of four or five people who are important to you.

B. Choose the person you want to write about and circle that person's name.

C. Brainstorm as many words or phrases as you can about that person. Remember, when you brainstorm, try to write down as many ideas as possible. Use any words from the photo page that you want. Also, use the illustrations on pages 26-27 to help you describe his or her appearance.

ORGANIZE YOUR IDEAS

A. Sara wants to write about her little brother, Adam. She brainstormed about him and wrote this list of ideas. Read her list.

BRAINSTORMING		
	Adam	
I miss him!	goes to school every day	smart
little brother	I had his teacher before.	follows my teenage brother around
7 years old	I wrote to him yesterday.	cheerful
funny—plays jokes	drives him crazy	laughs a lot
short for his age	2 brothers, 1 sister	curly, dark brown hair
the youngest	brown eyes	plays soccer after school
a little fat	sweet	loves school

Sara wrote many different ideas about Adam. To write her paragraph, she needs to organize them. One way to organize ideas is by *category*. A category is a group of similar things. Look at the list that follows. What three categories did Sara use to organize her information?

Adam		
APPEARANCE	LIFE	CHARACTER
curly, dark brown hair	little brother	funny—plays jokes
brown eyes	7 years old	sweet—loves animals
a little fat	laughs a lot	smart—loves school
short for his age	the youngest	cheerful—talks and laughs a lot
missing a few teeth	goes to school every day	
	follows my brother around	
	drives him crazy	
	plays soccer after school	

Questions

Which words or phrases did Sara write down when she brainstormed but not when she organized her ideas? Why were they left out?

She also added some ideas. What are they?

What Do They Look Like?

Age   young   middle-aged   old

Shape   fat   heavy   slim   thin

Height   tall   medium   short

Hair   long   short   straight   curly   wavy

Face

round   long   square   oval

Eyes

dark brown   light brown   blue   green   gray

W o m e n
Appearance

beautiful   ugly

M e n
Appearance

ugly   handsome

Features

pierced ear

Features

beard   moustache

B. Now organize your brainstorming ideas in the same way on your paper. Take out any irrelevant ideas. Add more ideas if you want to.

C. You have three categories of information. When you write, is it better to write about one category first, then the next, and then the third? Or is it better to mix up the information and not keep the categories together? Decide the best way to organize the information for your paragraph.

WRITE

Get comfortable, relax, and think about your important person. Then write a paragraph about that person. Remember, you will write your paragraph two more times, so don't worry about every mistake.

A. You learned in Chapter 1 that every paragraph in English is about one main idea. Here is the paragraph that Sara wrote about Adam. What is the main idea of her paragraph? Where does she tell you the main idea?

Adam

Adam is a delightful little boy. My wonderful little brother. He is seven years old and the youngest in our family. He has dark, curly hair. And big brown eyes. He often smiles. Then, you can see that he is missing some teeth. He short for his age and a little fat. Adam goes to school every day he often plays soccer with his friends after school. They aren't very good, but they have a lot of fun. Also loves to follow my teenage brother around. That drives my brother crazy! Adam is a sweet little boy, he really loves animals. Sometimes, he tries to take care of hurt, wild animals. Also, very smart. He loves school, and he gets good grades. I love him because he is funny and cheerful, too. He talks and laughs a lot, he makes everyone laugh with his silly jokes. Now, I in this country, and I miss him very much.

The Topic Sentence

The sentence that tells us the main idea is called the **topic sentence.** It is usually the first sentence in a paragraph.

All of the other sentences in the paragraph talk about the topic sentence. They must all be *relevant* to the topic sentence. These other sentences are called **supporting sentences.** Supporting sentences help the reader understand the main idea by giving more information about it.

The supporting sentences need to be in a good order. Supporting sentences about similar ideas should be together in the paragraph. What order of categories did Sara use? What category did she write about first, second, and third?

Exercise 1

Each group of sentences has one topic sentence and three supporting sentences. Write a *T* next to the topic sentence.

A.

_____ 1. Amy always understands me.

_____ 2. Amy is special to me.

_____ 3. I think Amy is beautiful.

_____ 4. Amy dances like a wild woman.

(If you see these sentences in a paragraph, you will not see *Amy* in every sentence. The writer will use *she* after the first sentence.)

B.

_____ 1. To me, my father is a great man.

_____ 2. My father is an excellent lawyer.

_____ 3. My father loves his family.

_____ 4. My father always has time for me.

C.

_____ 1. Chris likes to have a good time.

_____ 2. Chris is short and has wavy, brown hair.

_____ 3. Chris is one of my favorite people.

_____ 4. Every day, Chris runs several miles.

Exercise 2

Read the paragraph on the next page. Then read the sentences that follow the paragraph. Check (✔) the sentences that are good topic sentences for this paragraph.

My Grandmother

_____. She was born 77 years ago in England. When she was a baby, her family moved to the United States. After high school, she worked in a bakery until she married my grandfather. She can still make delicious cakes! My grandfather died five years ago, so she lives with us now. My grandmother has a short temper, but she never gets angry with me. She always listens to me and helps me with my problems.

_____ 1. My grandmother is tall and thin.

_____ 2. I think my grandmother is a wonderful person.

_____ 3. An important person in my life is my grandmother.

_____ 4. My grandmother had five children.

_____ 5. Let me tell you about Grandma.

_____ 6. My grandmother can make me laugh when I am sad.

Exercise 3

Read the following student paragraph. Then read the sentences that follow the paragraph on the next page. Check (✔) the sentences that are good topic sentences for this paragraph.

Capito

_____. He's a medium-size Labrador retriever with short, yellow hair and a long tail. In the house, he is always with me. When he comes to me, he hits everything with his tail. He also likes to come with me for a walk or a drive. Capito loves water. He loves to swim, play in the rain, and even play with the water in his bowl. He is a good pupil. He likes to learn, and he knows a lot of commands. Also, Capito is very gentle. He runs after cats, but he doesn't touch them.

_____ 1. Capito is my dog and my friend.

_____ 2. Capito's face is big and square.

_____ 3. My dog is seven years old.

_____ 4. Capito is a lovable dog.

_____ 5. Dogs are good pets.

_____ 6. Capito is my wonderful pet.

Exercise 4

Write a good topic sentence for this paragraph.

A Teacher to Remember

_____

He was a tall, thin man with red hair, and he wore thick glasses. In the classroom, he was always moving. He never sat still. When he was teaching, he always walked around, swung his arms, or tapped his feet. Mr. Jenkins put his energy into teaching us literature and drama at my high school. He was an excellent teacher. He taught us to love literature. Also, he helped the students give two school plays every year. Mr. Jenkins cared a lot about his students too. He always had time to talk to students about their problems. I hope that I can be like him when I am a teacher.

REVISION REVIEW

Read the following student paragraph. Think about the things you have learned, and answer these questions with your class.

1. What do you like about this paragraph?
2. Is the paragraph about one main idea?
3. Is there a good topic sentence?
4. Are all of the supporting sentences relevant to the main idea?
5. Are the supporting sentences in a good order?

My Friend

Eun Hee and I met in high school. When I left Korea, she cried. Eun Hee works at General Hospital, and she is never absent from work. She likes to take care of the patients, but she doesn't like the doctors. She says they don't respect the nurses. One doctor always shouts at the nurses. On the weekends, she goes to the mountains or visits an interesting place. Eun Hee is very active. If there is something that she wants to do, she does it. She is cheerful and talkative. When I had a long face and was sad, she talked cheerfully to me. Eun Hee is tall and too thin. She has small, brown eyes and long, curly, dark brown hair. She looks like Olive Oyl. Olive Oyl is Popeye's girlfriend in cartoons. Sometimes, when my friends and I were serious, she told jokes to us. I love her, and I want to see her again soon.

Exchange your paper with a partner. Read your partner's paragraph and answer these questions about it.

1. What do you like about your partner's paper? Put a star (★) next to any word, sentence, or idea that you like.

2. Is there anything that you do not understand? Put a question mark (?) in the margin next to any sentence that you do not understand.

3. Is there a topic sentence about the main idea? Under your partner's paragraph write *3* and answer *yes* or *no*.

4. Do all of the supporting sentences give information about the topic sentence? Are there any irrelevant sentences? Put parentheses ( ) around any irrelevant sentences.

5. Are there some sentences about the person's life, appearance, and character? Under your partner's paragraph write *5* and answer *yes* or *no*.

6. On the bottom of your partner's paper, write one question about the paragraph. Ask about something your partner did not tell about the important person.

Get your paper back from your partner. Talk to your partner about your paper.

- If there are any question marks on your paper, write those sentences more clearly. Ask your teacher or your partner for help if you need it.
- Answer your partner's question about your important person. Add that information to your paper if you want to.
- Think about the questions in Revision Review. Do you need to make any other changes to your own paper?

Rewrite your paragraph with your changes and new information in it.

EDIT

A. Reread the paragraph about Adam. Many of the sentences have problems. We will look at these problems and how to fix them.

Adam

(1) Adam is a delightful little boy. (2) My wonderful little brother. (3) He is seven years old and the youngest in our family. (4) He has dark, curly hair. (5) And big brown eyes. (6) He often smiles. (7) Then, you can see that he is missing some teeth. (8) He short for his age and a little fat. (9) Adam goes to school every day he often plays soccer with his friends after school. (10) They aren't very good, but they have a lot of fun. (11) Also loves to follow my teenage brother around. (12) That drives my brother crazy! (13) Adam is a sweet little boy, he really loves animals. (14) Sometimes, he tries to take care of hurt, wild animals. (15) Also, very smart. (16) He loves school, and he gets good grades. (17) I love him because he is funny and cheerful, too. (18) He talks and laughs a lot, he makes everyone laugh with his silly jokes. (19) Now, I in this country, and I miss him very much.

In Chapter 1, you learned that every English sentence has a _____ and a _____. The _____ usually comes before the _____. A sentence with one subject and verb group is called a **simple sentence.** There are two kinds of problems that a simple sentence can have.

Fragment

Every sentence must have both a subject and a verb. If a sentence does not have both of them, it is called a **fragment.** "Fragment" means "broken piece." A sentence fragment is only a piece of a sentence, not a whole sentence.

A fragment can have one of three problems.

1. No subject
   Also loves to follow my teenage brother around.
2. No verb
   He short for his age and a little fat.
3. No subject or verb
   And big brown eyes.

Exercise 1

Read the following sentence fragments and circle the problem for each.

1. My wonderful old grandmother.

   No subject   No verb   No subject or verb

2. Every morning of her long life.

   No subject   No verb   No subject or verb

3. Fixes breakfast for her family.

   No subject   No verb   No subject or verb

4. A cigarette always in her mouth.

   No subject   No verb   No subject or verb

5. Often worry about her.

   No subject   No verb   No subject or verb

Exercise 2

Write *F* next to the fragments and *S* next to the complete sentences.

_____ 1. My niece is a special person in my life.

_____ 2. Only nine months old.

_____ 3. Her silky, black hair.

_____ 4. Likes to play at three in the morning!

_____ 5. I love her.

Ways to Fix a Fragment

1. Add a subject or a verb.

   Fragment: *Also loves to follow my teenage brother around.*

   Sentence: *<u>He</u> also loves to follow my teenage brother around.*

   Fragment: *He short for his age and a little fat.*

   Sentence: *He <u>is</u> short for his age and a little fat.*

2. Add a subject and a verb.

   Fragment: *My wonderful little brother.*

   Sentence: *<u>He</u> <u>is</u> my wonderful little brother.*

3. Add the fragment to another sentence.

   Fragment: *And big brown eyes.*

   Sentence: *<u>He has dark, curly hair</u> and big brown eyes.*

Exercise 3

Look at the following pairs of sentences. In each pair, one sentence is a fragment. Change the fragment either by adding something to it or by joining it to the other sentence. There are several possible ways to fix each fragment. Write only one.

Example: An important person in my life is not a person. He a cat.

He is a cat.
_____

1. One night, he came to my door. And cried for food.

   _____

2. After that first night. Tramp has stayed with me.

   _____

3. Tramp is a large, gray cat. With one torn ear.

_____

4. He sleeps a lot during the day. And hunts at night.

_____

5. He tries to catch mice. Too fast for him.

_____

6. My cat and some of the neighborhood cats. They fight sometimes.

_____

7. In the evenings. Tramp watches TV with me.

_____

8. Day and night, he a good friend to me. He keeps me company.

_____

Run-on Sentence

A simple sentence has a subject and a verb.

1. _Adam is a sweet little boy._
      S   V

When you write a new subject and verb group, you must begin a new sentence.

2. _Adam is a sweet little boy. He really loves animals._
      S   V   S   V

If you do not begin a new sentence when you write a new subject and verb group, then you have a **run-on sentence**.

Some run-on sentences have no punctuation in them.

3. _Adam is a sweet little boy he really loves animals._

Some run-on sentences have a comma before the new subject.

4. _Adam is a sweet little boy, he really loves animals._

Both of these mistakes are run-on sentences.

Exercise 1

Write _RO_ next to the run-on sentences.

_____ 1. I want to own a company some day. I hope to be a good boss.

_____ 2. I remember my first boss, he was a terrible one.

_____ 3. He never listened to us. He only shouted.

_____ 4. He helped some workers a lot other workers got no help from him.

_____ 5. He also stole from the company and blamed the workers for it.

Ways to Fix a Run-on Sentence

To change a run-on sentence, make it into two simple sentences. Add a period at the end of the first subject and verb group.

Run-on: *Adam is a sweet little boy he really loves animals.*

Run-on: *Adam is a sweet little boy, he really loves animals.*

Sentence: *Adam is a sweet little boy. He really loves animals.*

Exercise 2

Change these run-on sentences.

1. A person important to me is my twin sister her name is Jody.

   _____

2. Jody and I are the same height, we have blonde hair and green eyes.

   _____

3. We enjoy the same things for example, we both love hot dogs and chess.

   _____

4. Jody understands me better than anyone, she knows me very well.

   _____

5. I can't live without my twin once a day, we call and talk on the telephone.

   _____

Exercise 3

In the paragraph on the next page, some of the sentences are run-ons. Add periods and take out commas to change the run-ons. The first one has been done for you.

```
                              Mac
                        W
     Mac is a special guy. /we have been friends for a long

time. Now we are at college together. Mac is tall and

very thin, my mother calls him "Stringbean." He has a

tough life. He takes classes during the day and drives

a taxi every night. His father drinks too much and

sometimes fights with his mother Mac tries to help her.

He also likes to have a good time. On his night off, he

goes out with his girlfriend, sometimes they drive to

the beach at three in the morning! He is amazing.
```

Exercise 4

Look again at the paragraph about Adam on page 33.

1. Underline all of the subjects and verbs.
2. Find the fragments and run-on sentences and change them.

B. To be an independent writer, you need to learn to find and fix your mistakes yourself.

   a. First, <u>underline</u> all of the subjects in your sentences and (circle) all of the verbs.

   b. Read your paper many times. Look for only one kind of mistake each time. For example, the first time you read your paper, ask yourself, "Does each sentence have a subject and a verb?" That time, do not look for fragments or verb mistakes. The next time you read it, look for a different kind of mistake.

   c. Use the following checklist to help you check your paragraph. Look for each kind of mistake one by one.

   d. Use *Quick Check* on page 137 to help you correct your mistakes.

Editing Checklist ☑

Look at each subject and verb group.

_____ 1. Does every sentence have a subject and verb?

_____ 2. Are there any fragments?

_____ 3. Are there any run-on sentences?

Look at the verbs.

_____ 4. Are all of the verbs in the correct tense?

_____ 5. Are all of the verbs in the correct form?

_____ 6. Do all of the verbs agree with their subjects?

Look at the sentences.

_____ 7. Do all of the sentences end with the correct punctuation?

_____ 8. Is each word spelled correctly?

Rewrite your paragraph in good form. To remember good form, look at page 21.

A Collage

A. Make a collage at home. On a strong piece of paper, paste pictures and things that tell about your important person. Use pictures from old magazines, newspapers, jar labels, pieces of string—anything! The collage should give the same information about the person that your paragraph does. Do *not* write your name or the name of your important person on the collage.

B. Bring your collage to school and give it to your teacher along with your paragraph. Do not show your collage to your classmates.

C. Your teacher will hang all of the paragraphs on one wall of the room, and the collages on another wall. The collages should be numbered.

D. Read all of the paragraphs and look at the collages. The goal is to match the collage with its paragraph. You can write the number of a collage under its matching paragraph.

E. Each student then tells which collage actually matches his or her paragraph.

CHAPTER 3

The Weekend!

The weekend begins on Friday night and ends on Sunday night. Our weekend lives are different from our weekday lives. Some people have time to relax and have fun. Other people must work at weekend jobs. Many people sleep late in the morning and stay up late at night. It is a time to do work around the house, go shopping—and go to parties!

What do you usually do on the weekend? In this chapter, you will think and write about that.

Picture This...

1. _____
_____
_____

2. _____
_____
_____

1. _____
_____
_____

2. _____
_____
_____

Talk about each photograph. Then write your answers to the questions.

1. What is happening in the photograph?
2. Do you do this on the weekend?

GET IDEAS

A. You have used brainstorming as one way to get ideas. Another way to get ideas is by *webbing*. A spider makes a web of connecting threads.

A writer can make a web of connecting ideas. As in brainstorming, the purpose of webbing is to write down as many ideas as possible.

Here is how to do it. In the center of your paper, write a word or a phrase giving the main idea of the paragraph that you will write. Draw a circle around it. Next, draw lines away from the circle, and at the ends of the lines write any words or phrases you can think of that are related to the main idea. Then, draw lines away from those words or phrases and write other ideas related to them.

Here is an example of webbing for the main idea *weekday*. This is what you would do if you wanted to get ideas for a paragraph about a weekday. Part of the web has been done for you. Draw more lines and add your own ideas.

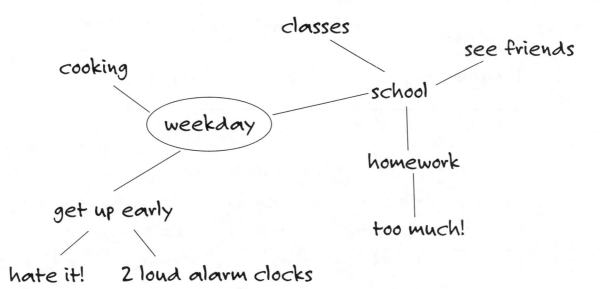

B. Get in a group with several other students. Talk about what you usually do on the weekend.

C. On your own, choose one weekend day, either Saturday or Sunday, and make a web for it. Write *Saturday* or *Sunday* in the center of a piece of paper. Draw a circle around it. Connect as many words or phrases to it as you can. Look back at the photo page for ideas.

ORGANIZE YOUR IDEAS

A. Look at your web for Saturday or Sunday. Circle the ideas you want to use. You can use all of them if you want.

B. Look at the words that you have circled. Many of them are probably about things that you do during that day. What do you do first? Put a *1* next to it. What do you do second? Put a *2* next to it. Do the same for all of the other circled words. When you finish, you will have the time order for your paragraph.

WRITE

Get comfortable, relax, and write your own paragraph about what you do either on Saturday or on Sunday. Use the ideas in your web.

REVISE

Here are two short paragraphs about Saturday. Read them and decide which is easier to understand.

Paragraph A

Saturday

Saturday is the worst day and the best day of the week for me. I usually wake up late. First, I take a shower, and then, I sometimes wash my car. After that, I eat lunch. I don't eat breakfast on Saturday because I get up late. After I eat lunch, I go to my uncle's store where I work. That is the start of a terrible time. It is very difficult to sell things because I cannot understand English. I am especially afraid of the telephone. I always make mistakes. While I am working in the store, I feel like I am walking in a hell. After work, I go back home. I eat dinner and then stay in my room to study or read. About ten o'clock, I call my girlfriend in my country. It is the happiest time of the week. If I could not call her, I would go back to my country. After I call my girlfriend, I go to bed and to sleep.

Paragraph B

Saturday

Saturday is the worst day and the best day of the week for me. I usually wake up late. I take a shower, and I sometimes wash my car. I eat lunch. I don't eat breakfast on Saturday because I get up late. I go to my uncle's store where I work. That is the start of a terrible time. It is very difficult to sell things because I cannot understand English. I am especially afraid of the telephone. I always make mistakes. While I am working in the store, I feel like I am walking in a hell. I go back home. I eat dinner and then stay in my room to study or read. About ten o'clock, I call my girlfriend in my country. It is the happiest time of the week. If I could not call her, I would go back to my country. I go to bed and to sleep.

You will probably agree that Paragraph A is easier to understand. Why? How is Paragraph A different from Paragraph B?

When you write your paragraph, you need to use words to tell the reader what you do first, second, and so on. Paragraph A does this, but Paragraph B does not. Which words in Paragraph A tell the time order? Here are some words that we use to tell the order that something happened in.

first	**after that**	**in the morning**	**at night**
next	**later**	**in the afternoon**	
then	**finally**	**in the evening**	

These words and phrases are called **transitions.** Transition means change. We use these transitions when we change to a new time in the paragraph.

Look back at Paragraph A. Notice how the transitions are punctuated. Also, notice that transitions are *not* the subject of the sentence.

Example: *First, I take a shower, and then, I sometimes wash my car.*
               s   s

After that, I eat lunch.
            s

Exercise 1

All of the transitions have been left out of the paragraph on the next page. Write in the transitions. Some sentences have several possible answers. Write only one. Be sure to add punctuation.

The Best Day of the Week

Sunday is my favorite day of the week. _____ I sleep a long time. _____ I get up and eat a huge breakfast. I read the newspaper while I eat. _____ I do some chores. My apartment is small, so it is easy to clean. I take my dirty clothes to a laundromat. _____ I call a friend, and we go shopping or to the gym. _____ we pick up a pizza and go back to my place to eat it. _____ we rent a video or watch a movie on TV. My friend goes home early because we both have classes on Monday. _____ I listen to music and finish my homework in the quiet night.

REVISION REVIEW

Read the following student paragraph. Think about the things you have already learned, and answer these questions with your class.

1. What do you like about this paragraph?
2. Is the paragraph about one main idea?
3. Is there a good topic sentence?
4. Are all of the supporting sentences relevant to the main idea?
5. Are the supporting sentences in a good order?
6. Did the writer use enough transitions?

My Sunday

This is about my Sunday. I usually wake up late, at 12 o'clock or 2 o'clock. Then, I take a shower before I eat lunch. But sometimes on Sunday morning, I wake up early. I play basketball with my friends at the university. We go to an Asian food store to buy food and the mall to buy clothes. My roommate buys a lot of clothes and CDs every week. I don't know why he does that. He doesn't need them. I always go to my aunt's house. My aunt, my cousins, and I eat lunch and talk to each other. In the afternoon, I usually go to a movie theater to watch a movie with my cousins. I go back to my dormitory. I do my homework and write in my journal in the evening. But first, I always talk on the phone to my family and friends. Then, my roommates and I listen to music and talk about the future in my dorm room. Finally, I organize my backpack before I go to bed. I always go to sleep early on Sunday night.

Reread your own paragraph and answer these questions about it.

1. Did you use any transitions to show the time order in your paragraph?
2. Do you need any more transitions?
3. Which transitions did you use? Write them here.

_____

_____

4. Look at your own paragraph and ask yourself the questions in the Revision Review. Do you need to make any changes?

Rewrite your paragraph. Make any changes you need to.

EDIT

Here is one student's paragraph about her favorite weekend day, Saturday.

Saturday

Saturday is my favorite day. I don't go to school. I get up late in the morning. First, I call my mother. We talk about my life. Next, I vacuum the apartment. My sister cooks us breakfast. I don't hate cooking. My sister is a better cook than I. After breakfast, I go shopping. I like shopping. I usually buy some clothes. In the afternoon, I meet my boyfriend. We go to interesting places such as Centennial Park, the beach under the Bay Bridge, and famous historic districts. I don't know my way in Baltimore. He guides me. I like walking. We walk together and talk to each other. Later, we eat dinner at a restaurant. He takes me home. Sometimes we watch a video. Other times we watch an old movie on TV. Then, he goes home. I get ready for bed and talk to my sister about the day. I am usually very tired. I go to sleep quickly. Then, my night of dreams begins.

All of the sentences in this paragraph are simple sentences. Remember that a simple sentence has _____ subject and verb group. Simple sentences are good ones, but your paper might sound boring if all of your sentences are simple sentences. To solve this problem, you can change some of the simple sentences to *compound* sentences.

Compound Sentences

Question: What do you get when you join hydrogen and oxygen?
Answer: a compound called *water:*   water = $H_2 + O$
Question: What do you get when you join two simple sentences?
Answer: a compound sentence

> compound sentence = simple sentence + simple sentence
>
> *I don't go to school, so I get up late in the morning.*
>   SIMPLE SENTENCE   +   SIMPLE SENTENCE

When a simple sentence is part of a compound sentence, the simple sentence has a different name. It is called an **independent clause.** A clause is any group of words with a subject and a verb. An *independent clause* is a clause that can stand by itself as a sentence.

A compound sentence is made of two independent clauses.

I don't go to school, so I get up late in the morning.
INDEPENDENT CLAUSE   +   INDEPENDENT CLAUSE

To join the independent clauses we use **coordinate conjunctions. A conjunction** is a word that joins things. A **coordinate conjunction** joins things that are the same, or equal. In a compound sentence, they join two independent clauses. Here are some coordinate conjunctions we use most often: *and, but, so,* and *or.*

▌ **And** shows added information.

Rob and Sara go to the library,   **and**   *they study for three hours.*
    INDEPENDENT CLAUSE   CC   INDEPENDENT CLAUSE

▌ **But** shows something different happens or the opposite.

I go to work on Saturday,   **but**   *I don't work on Sunday.*
    INDEPENDENT CLAUSE   CC   INDEPENDENT CLAUSE

▌ **So** shows the result of something.

Kim misses her family   **so**   *she calls them every weekend.*
INDEPENDENT CLAUSE   CC   INDEPENDENT CLAUSE

▌ **Or** shows something instead of something.

In the afternoon, I clean my room,   **or**   *I read a book.*
    INDEPENDENT CLAUSE   CC   INDEPENDENT CLAUSE

Question: What punctuation is used in a compound sentence? Where is it used?

Exercise 1

Diana asked her classmates about their Sunday activities. Match the beginning of each answer with its ending.

____ 1. Tony works late on Saturday night,

a. and she drinks it on the balcony.

____ 2. Rosa takes her children to the park,

b. and they go out to eat after church.

____ 3. Shu Fen relaxes in her room all day,

c. but on a rainy day, she watches TV.

____ 4. Yoji and his girlfriend go to a movie,

d. so he sleeps late on Sunday.

____ 5. In the morning, Lisa makes coffee,

e. or he plays tennis with a friend.

____ 6. On a good day, Maria takes a walk,

f. but she studies at night.

____ 7. Hwa Sun goes to church with her family,

g. so her children love Sunday.

____ 8. After lunch, Ahmed works on his car,

h. or they rent a video.

Exercise 2

Join these two simple sentences into one compound sentence. Use a coordinate conjunction (*and, but, so,* and *or*). Be sure to punctuate the sentence correctly.

1. I like to stay up late to watch old movies on TV. My husband likes to go to bed early.

_____

_____

2. Ken washes cars on Saturday. He delivers pizzas on Sunday.

_____

3. Carol loves art. She goes to the museum every Saturday.

_____

4. Christy and Ben go dancing Saturday night. They go to a wrestling match.

_____

_____

Exercise 3

Finish these compound sentences with your own words.

1. I like to sleep late, but _____

2. We don't have school on the weekend, so _____

3. My mother cooks a big meal on Sunday, or _____

4. On Saturday afternoon, I call my best friend, and _____

Exercise 4

The following paragraph has no punctuation. Add the periods (.) and the commas (,). Some of the sentences are simple and some are compound. The first one has been done for you.

My Saturdays

My Saturdays are very interesting. I live by the ocean and I work there for a very old woman in the past she loved to stand on the beach and watch the sunrise but now she is too old to leave her house my job is to take pictures of the sunrise for her every Saturday morning first I leave my house in the dark and I walk to the beach with my camera then I take lots of pictures of the sunrise I am often sleepy but I love to be near the ocean in the morning next I go home and eat a big breakfast after that I develop the pictures in my own darkroom in the afternoon I take the pictures to the old woman and we talk about the ocean she pays me so I have money to go out with my boyfriend at night we go to a baseball game or we have fun at an amusement park later we walk by the ocean in the moonlight my Saturday begins and ends by the ocean

---

Exercise 5

Look at the following paragraph about Saturday again. With a partner, try to join some of the simple sentences to make compound sentences.

Saturday

(1) Saturday is my favorite day. (2) I don't go to school. (3) I get up late in the

morning. (4) First, I call my mother. (5) We talk about my life. (6) Next, I vacuum

the apartment. (7) My sister cooks us breakfast. (8) I don't hate cooking. (9) My

sister is a better cook than I. (10) After breakfast, I go shopping. (11) I like

shopping. (12) I usually buy some clothes. (13) In the afternoon, I meet my

boyfriend. (14) We go to interesting places such as Centennial Park, the beach

under the Bay Bridge, and famous historic districts. (15) I don't know my way in

Baltimore. (16) He guides me. (17) I like walking. (18) We walk together and talk

to each other. (19) Later, we eat dinner at a restaurant. (20) He takes me home.

(21) Sometimes we watch a video. (22) Other times we watch an old movie on TV.

(23) Then, he goeshome. (24) I get ready for bed and talk to my sister about the

day. (25) I am usually very tired. (26) I go to sleep quickly. (27) Then, my night of

dreams begins.

Now look at your own paragraph about the weekend. Did you write any compound sentences? Can you make any more compound sentences?

To check your paragraph, use the Editing Checklist that follows.

Remember

a. First, underline all of the subjects in your sentences and circle all of the verbs.

b. Read your paper many times. Look for only one kind of mistake each time. For example, the first time you read your paper, ask yourself, "Does each sentence have a subject and a verb?" That time, do not look for fragments or verb mistakes. The next time you read it, look for a different kind of mistake.

c. Use this checklist to help you check your paragraph. Look for each kind of mistake one by one.

d. Use *Quick Check* on page 137 to help you fix your mistakes.

Editing Checklist ✔

Look at each subject and verb group.

_____ 1. Does every sentence have a subject and verb?

_____ 2. Are there any fragments?

_____ 3. Are there any run-on sentences?

Look at the verbs.

_____ 4. Do all of the verbs agree with their subjects?

_____ 5. Are all of the verbs in the correct form?

Look at the punctuation and capitalization.

_____ 6. Do all of the sentences end with the correct punctuation?

_____ 7. Is there a comma after each transition?

_____ 8. Is there a comma in each compound sentence?

_____ 9. Does each sentence begin with a capital letter?

_____ 10. Are Saturday and Sunday capitalized?

Look at the words.

_____ 11. Is each word spelled correctly?

Rewrite your paragraph in good form. To remember good form, look at page 21.

A Step Further...

The Perfect Weekend

A. You wrote about your real weekend. Now you will think about your perfect weekend. Imagine that you can go anywhere you want, do anything you want, and be with any person you want. What will you do? Where will you go? Who will you be with? Unfortunately, you have only one weekend, from Friday night to Sunday night.

B. Write down your plan for a perfect weekend. Include what you will do, where you will go, and who you will be with for the whole weekend. You do not need to write a paragraph. You will use your plan as notes for talking.

C. Your class should divide into small groups. In your groups, take turns describing your perfect weekend. Listen to each other and ask questions.

CHAPTER 4

A Scary or Funny Experience

Sometimes when friends and family are at a party, sitting around the dinner table, or just relaxing together, stories are told. "I remember when...," someone begins, and everyone ends up laughing. "I'll never forget...," another person says, and everyone shivers with fear. All of us have stories from our own lives. Some of the stories are funny and make us laugh. Others are scary and make us feel afraid for a moment. In this chapter, you will write a story from your own life, either something funny or something scary.

Picture This...

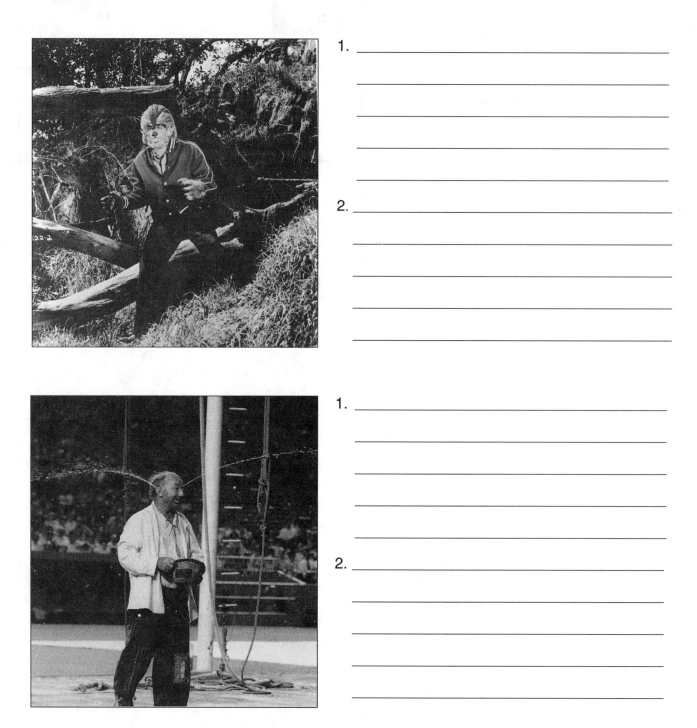

1. _____

_____

_____

_____

_____

2. _____

_____

_____

_____

_____

1. _____

_____

_____

_____

_____

2. _____

_____

_____

_____

_____

Talk about each photograph. Then write your answers to the questions.

1. What is happening in the photograph?
2. How does the person in the photograph feel?

GET IDEAS

Get into small groups. Each person will tell either a scary story or a funny story from his or her own life. It could be a memory from your childhood, about your family, about your friends, or about your time in school. It could be a ghost story that you have heard or a frightening experience from your own life. If you like, you can tell both a funny story and a scary story. As members of your group tell their stories, be sure to ask a lot of questions to help them think of lots of ideas to include later in their paragraphs.

ORGANIZE YOUR IDEAS

A. Find a partner from a different group than the one you were just in. Exchange textbooks with your partner.

B. Imagine that you are a newspaper reporter. Your assignment is to get information about your partner's scary or funny experience. Ask your partner the questions that follow, and write down his or her answers in his or her textbook.

1. Who was there?

2. When did it happen?

3. Where did it happen?

4. What happened? (a summary)

5. Why did it happen?

6. How did you and the others feel?

A Scary or Funny Experience

C. Get your textbook back from your partner. Read what your partner wrote in your book. Is everything accurate? Do you need to add anything? Think about the best way to tell your story.

WRITE

Write a paragraph telling your funny or scary story. You want the readers to be able to picture the story in their minds as they read it. Try to include a lot of information to help the readers do this.

REVISE

A. Here is one student's story. It is an interesting story, but it leaves you with many questions. After you read the story, write some questions that you have about the story. Use the space following the story.

Paragraph A

> ### A Scary and Funny Experience
>
> I remember a time that was funny for me but scary for my sister. My sister was in her bedroom trying to sleep. I decided to make some strange noises. She couldn't sleep, so she called my mother. When my mother came, I stopped. My mother said, "I don't hear anything except the wind outside," and she went downstairs. I started again. My sister spoke to herself and to the noises. After that, she called my mother again. My mother shouted at the spirits too, and then she went downstairs again. Later, I couldn't keep quiet anymore, so I laughed. Then, my sister understood that I had made the noises.

_____

_____

_____

The writer rewrote the paragraph with much more information in it. Read the new paragraph and see if your questions have been answered.

Paragraph B

A Scary and Funny Experience

I remember a time that was funny for me but scary for my sister. It was about seven years ago, on a very dark night without a moon and with a lot of wind. My younger sister was in her bedroom, trying to sleep. I decided to go to the attic over her room and make some noises. I made ghost sounds, banged on the floor, and howled like a dog. My sister couldn't sleep, and I could hear her moving around in her room. Finally, she called my mother. When my mother came, I stopped. My mother listened. Then, she said, " I don't hear anything except the wind outside," and she returned downstairs to watch TV. After a few minutes, I started again. My sister was very nervous. She spoke to herself, and she told the ghost or animal or maybe spirits to go away. It was very funny, so it was very difficult for me not to laugh. After that, she called my mother again. This time my mother came with a long stick. She shouted at the spirits so that my sister wouldn't worry. But my mother didn't believe in the spirits, and soon returned to the TV.

After about one hour and thirty minutes, I couldn't keep quiet anymore. It was too funny. I started to laugh, and then my sister understood that I had made the noises. She was very angry. She shouted at me to come down from the attic. When I did, she said, "I can't sleep now because of you. You have to stay up all night with me." The next morning, my mother found us together. We were sitting on the floor, back to back, and we were sleeping.

Details

The second draft of the paragraph is much more interesting than the first because it contains many more **details.** *Details* are specific pieces of information that help us to understand a general idea better.

Paragraph A: I decided to make some strange noises.

Paragraph B: I decided to go to the attic over her room and make some noises. I made ghost sounds, banged on the floor, and howled like a dog.

There are different kinds of details.

1. **"Reporter" details**—This information answers the questions that reporters ask: *who, what, when, where, why,* and *how.*

   It was about seven years ago, on a very dark night without a moon and with a lot of wind.

2. **Sense details**—This is information about what you see, hear, smell, touch, and taste.

   My sister couldn't sleep, and I could hear her moving around in her room.

3. **Emotion details**—This is information about how the writer and the people in the paragraph feel.

   My sister was very nervous.

Look again at Paragraph B. Find other places where details were added to give the reader a clearer picture of the story. What kinds of details are they?

B. Now you will read each other's scary and funny experiences. Enjoy the stories and think about other details that you would like to know.

   1. Get into small groups.
   2. Your teacher will collect all of the papers, and then give each group some papers written by people not in that group.
   3. Each person in the group will read all of the papers. For each paper, follow these directions.
      a. What do you like about the story? Put a star (★) next to a word, sentence, or detail that you like.
      b. If you do not understand a sentence, put a question mark (?) next to that sentence.
      c. At the bottom of the paper, write one question about the story. Ask for more details about something in the paragraph. **You must write one question on each paper.** Do not ask a question about grammar.

   4. After all the groups are finished, you will get back your paper. If there are any question marks on it, think of a way to write those sentences more clearly. Ask your teacher or another student if you need help. Then, answer the questions on the bottom of your paper.

REVISION REVIEW

Read the following student paragraph. Think about the things you have learned, and answer these questions with your class.

1. What do you like about this paragraph?
2. Is the paragraph about one main idea?
3. Is there a good topic sentence?
4. Are all of the supporting sentences relevant to the main idea?
5. Are the supporting sentences in a good order?
6. Did the writer use enough transitions?
7. Did the writer give enough details?

A Scary Story

I remember about ten years ago when I stayed with some friends in my country. We were next to an old, empty house. We were talking about ghosts. Suddenly, someone said to me, "If you can go inside that house, I will give you 300 dollars. I thought about it. He gave me 300 dollars, and I went to the house. After I went inside the house, I was very scared because I had heard about this house. I was looking to the left and to the right because I don't like looking at anything scary. I got out of the house. I said, "Thank you, my God!" I didn't like that adventure, but I needed money.

C. Look at your own paper and ask yourself the questions in the Revision Review. Do you need to make any changes? Also, if they will make your story better, add the details that the other students asked for and any other details that you would like.

 Rewrite your paragraph.

Sentence Problem: Run-on Sentences

Remember   A compound sentence is made of _____ simple sentences. In a compound sentence, the simple sentences are called _____ clauses. There are usually only _____ of them in one compound sentence. The clauses are joined by a coordinate _____. A comma is written after the _____ independent clause.

Compare these sentences with the description of a compound sentence. Do these sentences fit the description? Talk about why or why not.

1. People have always talked about ghosts, and many books have been written about them, but people cannot agree on their existence.
2. Some people believe in ghosts others laugh at the idea, other people just aren't sure.
3. One student saw a ghost, and he'll never forget the experience he believes in them now.

Something to Remember

In academic writing, a compound sentence usually does not have more than two independent clauses. If it does, it is probably a **run-on sentence.**

Exercise 1

Read this student's story. Decide if the sentences are run-ons or not. Write *RO* above the run-on sentences.

A Visit

1. _____   2. _____

One night in my country, I couldn't sleep. I was alone in my bedroom, and my

3. _____

brother and sister were sleeping in their rooms. Outside, the weather was not

4. _____

good. It was raining hard my room was dark, and it was about three o'clock in

5. _____   6. _____

the morning. I prayed to God, and I wished for sleep. Suddenly, I saw a young

---

woman with long, black hair in front of me, and soft light was coming from

7. _____

her, so I could see her clearly. She gave me a smile, but she was floating

8. _____

above the floor. I was scared at the sight, I couldn't do anything, then, she

9. _____

started to laugh. I turned the light on with a big effort, but she disappeared

in front of me I went to the living room and sat there until morning.

10. _____

Even today, I can't forget that experience, and I hope she will never bother

me again.

Ways to Fix a Run-on Sentence

Change the run-on sentence into two or more good sentences. First, find all of the independent clauses and coordinate conjunctions in a sentence. Then, decide where to put in one or more periods to make several sentences from one run-on sentence. Add or take out coordinate conjunctions where you need to. There is usually more than one way to fix a run-on sentence. You can decide which way you like best.

1. Run-On

People have always talked about ghosts, and many books have been written about them, but people cannot agree on their existence.

Sentence

a. *People have always talked about ghosts. Many books have been written about them, but people cannot agree on their existence.*

OR

b. *People have always talked about ghosts, and many books have been written about them. But people cannot agree on their existence.*

2. Run-On

Some people believe in ghosts others laugh at the idea, other people just aren't sure.

Sentence

a. *Some people believe in ghosts. Others laugh at the idea. Other people just aren't sure.*

OR

b. *Some people believe in ghosts, but others laugh at the idea. Other people just aren't sure.*

OR

c. *Some people believe in ghosts. Others laugh at the idea, but other people just aren't sure.*

3. Run-On

One student saw a ghost, and he'll never forget the experience he believes in them now.

Sentence

One student saw a ghost, and he'll never forget the experience. He believes in them now.

Exercise 2

Look back at the sentences in Exercise 1. Change the run-on sentences by adding periods and capital letters.

Exercise 3

This student's paragraph is made of both simple and compound sentences, but there are many run-on sentences in it. Correct the run-on sentences by adding periods and capital letters and by removing some commas.

A Funny Story

A funny thing happened to my family three years ago. One evening, my parents, my brother, and I went to see a movie. After that, we went to eat dinner at a restaurant, we took a long time there. so we came back home about 12 o'clock. I opened the front door, I was very surprised. Somebody had scattered everything in my house. Books and records were on the floor, and the sofa was torn up. At that time, I heard a strange noise from my room, and I was sure that there was somebody in my room, and I wanted to be a hero, so I told my family, "Please, watch out. I will check my room." I walked slowly and quietly to my room and opened my door carefully. Suddenly, something ran out the window it was a wild cat. We realized that the cat had scattered everything in our house. I had forgotten to close the window. Then, we all laughed together.

Exercise 4

This student's story has both simple and compound sentences, but there are many run-on sentences in it. Change the run-on sentences by adding periods and capital letters and by removing some commas.

The student wrote about a terrible experience that happened in Texas. In 1987, an 18-month-old girl named Jessica fell down a well. Her rescuers had to drill a hole next to the well to reach her. The student imagined that she was Jessica and wrote the story from Jessica's point of view.

Jessica's Terrible Experience

When I was only 18 months old, something terrible happened to me. One day, while I was playing outside with some other children, I fell into a well, a deep well. At first, I didn't know what happened, I asked myself, "Why is it so dark? Where is my mommy?" After a few minutes, I heard my mom call me, "Jessica, Jessica, where are you?" Her voice sounded very worried then, I knew I was in the well. I began to feel pain because my body had hit on the rocky sides of the well. I cried and called my mom until I slept.

After a long time, I woke up, I was still in the well, I started to hear a loud noise. I didn't know what it was, but I thought maybe it was Superman. He was coming to save my life. I remembered the cartoons, Superman always saves people's lives. When I thought about that, I wasn't scared anymore. I even felt a little happy because I would see Superman. Finally, I saw him, but he forgot to wear his Superman clothes he forgot to wear his underwear outside. However, I believe he was my Superman. He took me up to see my mommy and daddy. They were both crying, and I cried, too. I was rescued!

Use the Editing Checklist to check your paragraph for run-on sentences and other problems.

Remember

a. First, <u>underline</u> all of the subjects in your sentences and ⟨circle⟩ all of the verbs.
b. Read your paper many times. Look for only one kind of mistake each time. For example, the first time you read your paper, ask yourself, "Does each

---

A Scary or Funny Experience

sentence have a subject and a verb?" That time, do not look for fragments or verb mistakes. The next time you read it, look for a different kind of mistake.

c. Use this checklist to help you check your paragraph. Look for each kind of mistake one by one.

d. Use *Quick Check* on page 137 to help you fix your mistakes.

Editing Checklist ✔

Look at each sentence.

_____ 1. Does every sentence have a subject and verb?

_____ 2. Are there any fragments?

_____ 3. Are there any run-on sentences?

Look at the verbs.

_____ 4. Do all of the verbs agree with their subjects?

_____ 5. Are all of the verbs in the correct tense?

_____ 6. Are all of the verbs in the correct form?

Look at the punctuation and capitalization.

_____ 7. Do all of the sentences end with the correct punctuation?

_____ 8. Is there a comma after each transition?

_____ 9. Is there a comma in each compound sentence?

Look at the words.

_____ 10. Is each word spelled correctly?

Rewrite your paragraph in good form. To remember good form, look at page 21.

A Radio Program

A. Get into several small groups. Everyone in each group will read the stories of everyone else in the group. Each group will choose one story to rewrite as a radio program.

B. Each group will make their story into a script for a radio program. It might be a drama, a news program, or any other kind of program. It might include commercials. It should include sound effects.

C. Each group should perform their radio program on cassette tape and bring the tape to class.

D. The class will listen to the radio programs together. If you like, the class can read the paragraphs first.

CHAPTER 5

Holidays

Holidays! They are different from all other days of the year. When we hear that word, we think of special food, clothes, and activities. We can close our eyes and remember certain sights, smells, sounds, and tastes. Most of all, we remember good times with our family and friends.

Picture This...

1. _____

   _____

   _____

2. _____

   _____

   _____

3. _____

   _____

   _____

Talk about the photograph. Then write your answers to the questions.

1. What is the name of the holiday?
2. What is happening in the photograph?
3. Do you celebrate the same or a similar holiday?

GET IDEAS

A. Think about the holidays in your country, and choose your favorite.

B. Write the name of the holiday in the middle of a piece of paper. Draw a circle around it and make a web of ideas, as you did in Chapter 3. Think about the things that you do and also the sights, sounds, smells and tastes of the holiday. Use any of the ideas from the photo page that you like.

ORGANIZE YOUR IDEAS

To organize the information in your web, fill out the chart below. Use the words and phrases from your web, and add more ideas if you need to.

Holiday: _____

What do you do, see, hear, smell, and taste...

1. before the day of the holiday to prepare for it?

2. in the morning on the day of the holiday?

3. in the afternoon?

4. in the evening?

5. at night?

C. Now form small groups. Try to be in a group with students from other countries.

1. Use your chart and talk to the other students about your favorite holiday.
2. Answer their questions, and write down any more information that you forgot on the chart.
3. Listen to the other students, and ask them questions about their holidays.

WRITE

Use the information in your chart to write a paragraph about your favorite holiday.

REVISE

In English, a paragraph has three parts: a beginning, a middle, and an end. So far we have talked about the beginning and the middle. The beginning tells the reader the main idea and is called the _____ sentence. The middle of a paragraph gives more information about the main idea. The sentences are called _____ sentences.

The end of a paragraph, which is the last sentence of the paragraph, is called the **conclusion.** The conclusion is not just another supporting sentence. It has a separate job to do. The conclusion can:

1. remind the reader of the main idea—to do this, it repeats the topic sentence in different words.
2. give the writer's feelings or opinions about the ideas in the paragraph.
3. do both of those things.

Read the following two student paragraphs. Pay particular attention to the conclusions.

Paragraph A

Eid Al Fitr

My favorite holiday of the year is Eid Al Fitr. It is the most famous holiday of the Moslem religion, and it comes after Ramadan. At the end of Ramadan before Al Eid, people prepare for the holiday. They go to the market to buy some new clothes and some sweets to eat. Mothers and daughters also clean the house. On the morning of Eid Al Fitr, people go to the mosque to pray. After that, we eat a huge breakfast with the family.

Children get money from the older people to buy toys. In the afternoon, people go to visit each other to wish each other a happy Eid. Families also go to eat in restaurants. Then, they go and have a good time on picnics. In the evening, people celebrate together until midnight. Finally, we go to sleep because we had woken up early on that day. Eid Al Fitr is the best day of the year for me.

Paragraph B

Chusak

Chusak is the most famous holiday in Korea. My family prepares many things the day before Chusak. First, we get up early in the morning. Then, we buy food and make special dishes for the next day. We always make "Songpyon." It is a traditional rice cake. After that, we clean our house. At the end of the day, we go to bed early because we have to get up early the next morning. On this holiday morning, we perform a sacrificial rite to our ancestors. After that, we eat the rite food together. In the afternoon, we usually visit my father's sister. We don't often visit her, so we talk to each other for a long time. We also play traditional games together such as "Yut." We spend the rest of the day at her home. Finally, we go home and go to bed early to take a rest. I always feel happy and peaceful at the end of the day on Chusak.

Reread the conclusions to Paragraphs A and B. Do they remind the reader of the main idea or give the writer's feelings?

Exercise 1

Read the student paragraph on the next page. Then choose a good conclusion for it from the list following the paragraph. There are several good conclusions. Put a check (✔) next to all the good conclusions.

Happy New Year

   I like the New Year in Japan because it is very exciting. On the night of December 31, my friends and I go to a karaoke club. We are rowdy and have fun there. At about 12 A.M. we go to the temple because Japanese people have to pray to God for the New Year. There are a lot of people in the famous temples. When the time is past 12 A.M., all the people say "*Akemashite Omedetou Gozaimasu.*" That means "Happy New Year." After that, we go to the beach to watch the sunrise on New Year's Day. It is very, very beautiful. In the morning, we go home. When I arrive home, the house smells sweet because my mother has cooked a lot of good food. My family eats the delicious food together. After that, my family goes to my grandfather's house in the afternoon. My other relatives are there too. We say "Happy New Year" to my relatives. When the children wish the adults a happy new year, the adults give them money. I like this custom. In the evening, we talk to our relatives, go out with friends, and so on. We play card games at night, and we have to bet money. It's a lot of fun, but I sometimes lose. At midnight, we all go home. _____

_____ 1. I am exhausted, but very happy.

_____ 2. My grandmother has to clean up their house.

_____ 3. I take a bath before I go to bed.

_____ 4. I think that New Year is the most wonderful time of the year.

_____ 5. During the year, I always smile when I remember our New Year fun.

_____ 6. The next morning, I hate to get up.

Exercise 2

Does your paragraph have a conclusion? If not, write several conclusions. Then, choose the best one.

REVISION REVIEW

One student imagined a perfect day for herself. Read her paragraph. Think about the things you have learned and answer these questions with your class.

1. What do you like about this paragraph?
2. Is the paragraph about one main idea?
3. Is there a good topic sentence?
4. Are all of the supporting sentences relevant to the main idea?
5. Are the supporting sentences in a good order?
6. Did the writer use enough transitions?
7. Did the writer give enough details?
8. Does the paragraph have a good conclusion?

One Day in Kenya

One day I went to Kenya. I had a role with Harrison Ford in a film. The film took place in Kenya. First, I met Harrison Ford. It was exciting for me because he is a very famous actor. He is handsome and strong. In the morning, we began to make the film. In the movie, my best friend is Koko, a monkey. Koko was very clever, and he knew many words. I was a veterinarian in the film. There were a lot of animals: giraffes, monkeys, snakes, elephants, and lions. In the afternoon, we went to a place where the elephants live. We went there by jeep. It was a lot of fun. Then, I saw a lot of elephants. They were very big and slow and looked earnest. I liked them. We saw a snake while we were watching the elephants. It was ugly and dangerous. I was very afraid, and I screamed. A Kenyan man killed it. Later, we returned to the camp. After that, we took a break for dinner. We ate some Kenyan food and drank cold drinks. In the evening, I talked with Harrison Ford about the cinema. Then, the director congratulated me on my effort.

Look at your own paper and ask yourself the questions in the Revision Review. Do you need to make any more changes?

 Rewrite your paragraph. Make any changes you need to.

EDIT

Look at these sentences. What kind is each one? Write *S* next to the simple sentences. Write *C* next to the compound sentences. Write *D* next to the ones that are a different kind of sentence.

_____ 1. Independence Day is July 4th in the United States, so it is a national holiday.

_____ 2. My family and I spend the day at a lake near our house.

_____ 3 My younger sisters like to wear red, white, and blue clothes because those are the colors of the United States flag.

_____ 4. We also put an American flag on the picnic table.

_____ 5. After we eat lunch, my father rents a motorboat.

_____ 6. My youngest sister always begs to drive it, but he never lets her.

_____ 7. I always try to water-ski although I'm not very good at it.

_____ 8. We have a cookout with watermelon for dessert, and my sisters have fun spitting the seeds at each other.

_____ 9 When the day is over, we drive back to town to watch the fireworks.

_____ 10. The fireworks are beautiful but over too soon.

Complex Sentences

The sentences that are different are called **complex sentences**. A *complex sentence* has two or more clauses in it. Remember that a compound sentence is made of two *independent* clauses. A complex sentence is made of one independent clause and one or more **dependent clauses**. A dependent clause cannot stand by itself as a sentence. It must always be joined to an independent clause.

1. *After we eat lunch,* + *my father rents a motorboat.*
   DEPENDENT   INDEPENDENT

2. *I always try to water-ski* + *although I'm not very good at it.*
   INDEPENDENT   DEPENDENT

How can you identify a dependent clause? Remember that independent clauses are joined by a coordinate conjunction (*and, but, so, or*). A dependent clause begins with a subordinate conjunction. There are many subordinate conjunctions. The ones we use most often are listed here.

after	**if**
although	**since**
because	**when**
before	**while**

▌ **After**—at a later time

After we eat lunch, my father rents a motorboat.

▌ **Although**—but

My youngest sister always begs to drive the boat although my father never lets her.

▌ **Because**—tells why

My younger sisters like to wear red, white, and blue clothes because those are the colors of the flag of the United States.

▌ **Before**—at an earlier time

Before the sun sets, we find a high hill for watching the fireworks.

▌ **If** tells a possible situation.

If it rains on July 4th, we are all disappointed.

▌ **Since**—means the same as *because*

My younger sisters like to wear red, white,and blue clothes since those are the colors of the flag of the United States.

▌ **When**—at that time

When the day is over, we drive back to town to watch the fireworks.

▌ **While**—happening at the same time as the independent clause

While my sisters and I sunbathe, we watch the boys on the beach.

Exercise ▣1

An April Fool's Day Trick

Many countries have a special day for people to play tricks on each other for fun. In the United States and England, this happens on April 1st, called April Fool's Day. This trick is often played on people on April Fool's Day. (*Note:* In English, "fox" is both a wild animal and a family name.)

Match the beginning of each sentence with its ending.

_____ 1. Before Jim arrived at work,

a. while he was looking through his mail.

_____ 2. Please call Mr. Fox

b. after you get in.

_____ 3. If you don't know his number,

c. a coworker left a message on his desk.

_____ 4. Jim saw the message

d. it is 555-8720.

_____ 5. Jim called the number right away

a. he laughed at the joke.

_____ 6. When someone answered the phone,

b. since he wasn't busy.

_____ 7. The person on the phone laughed

c. Jim asked to speak to Mr. Fox.

_____ 8. Although Jim felt a little foolish,

d. because Jim's coworker had left the number for the zoo.

Exercise 2

Read this student paragraph and circle the correct subordinate conjunctions.

My Birthday

I think my birthday is the best holiday for me. *Before / While* my birthday comes, I usually call my friends and tell them about my birthday. I say to them the most important thing is to prepare a present *although / because* it is real important for me. In the morning on my birthday, I eat brown-seaweed soup. Every Korean eats brown-seaweed soup *after / when* it is their birthday. In the afternoon, I meet my friends, and we spend time together. *After / If* we go bowling, play pool, and so on, we go to a bar in the evening. My friends bring a cake and put on the candles. *Since / When* I blow them out, they push my head into the cake. Then, we eat the cake, and it tastes wonderful. At night, the terrible birthday ceremony starts. *When / Because* we go outside, my friends make a circle. *While / Before* I stand in the center of the circle, they hit me and throw eggs at me. The smell is incredible, but it isn't finished yet. They sprinkle flour on me. Then, they give me presents. *Although / After* the smell is terrible, the presents change my feelings. Anyway, I love my birthday *if / since* my friends and I have a very good time on that day.

Exercise 3

Read the following paragraph and fill in each blank with a subordinate conjunction that makes sense in that sentence. Some sentences may have more than one possible answer.

after   if   because   when

although   since   before   while

Summer Vacation

I think I am a typical student. (1) _____ I like school, I love vacations. (2) _____ I am bored in school, I like to daydream about my vacation plans. (3) _____ summer vacation is coming, I feel the happiest _____ it is the longest vacation. (4) _____ final exams are finished, I totally relax. I sleep late, eat at any time, and hang out with my friends. (5) Sometimes I have a part-time job _____ I am on vacation. (6) _____ I have a job, I have extra cash to have fun with. (7) Also, I go to the beach for awhile _____ my parents rent a cottage there. (8) _____ my vacation is over, I always visit my grandparents. (9) I love to visit them _____ they let me do whatever I like. Finally, summer ends, and it's back to school I go.

Notice that the dependent clause can come either before or after the independent clause.

After we eat lunch, my father rents a motorboat.

OR

My father rents a motorboat *after we eat lunch.*

Punctuation Rule

- If the dependent clause is at the beginning of the sentence, put a comma after the dependent clause.

  If it rains on July 4th, we are all disappointed.

- If the dependent clause is after the independent clause, do *not* put a comma after the independent clause.

  We are all disappointed *if it rains on July 4th.*

Exercise 4

Punctuate this paragraph.

Halloween

(1) Halloween is on October 31st when the weather is cool and crisp.
(2) Before the day comes children and many adults prepare costumes.
(3) Stores sell them but the best ones are homemade. (4) Children wear their costumes to go trick-or-treating in their neighborhoods after it gets dark. (5) The children knock on their neighbors' doors and then they shout, "Trick or treat!" (6) The people in the houses give them candy because the children will play tricks on them if they don't give them anything. (7) Although teenagers usually don't go trick-or-treating they still love to play tricks on people. (8) Adults often go to Halloween parties at night because they enjoy dressing in costumes and acting like children. (9) Parents also enjoy eating their children's trick-or-treat candy after the children are in bed! (10) When Halloween comes children of all ages are happy.

Exercise 5

Join each pair of sentences to make one complex sentence. Use a subordinate conjunction in each sentence, and punctuate the sentences correctly.

Halloween Revenge

1. Jason and Joe don't like their next door neighbor. He complains about their loud music.

   _____

   _____

2. Halloween came. They decided to play a trick on him.

   _____

   _____

3. Jason kept watch. Joe put toilet paper all over their neighbor's trees and bushes.

   _____

   _____

4. They hid behind some bushes. They finished.

   _____

   _____

5. The neighbor opened the door for some children. Jason and Joe were delighted to see the dismay on his face.

   _____

   _____

6. The neighbor went to work the next morning. He had to clean up the mess.

   _____

   _____

7. The neighbor asked lots of people. He never knew who had done it.

   _____

   _____

Exercise 6

Look at your paragraph. Do you have any complex sentences? Try to join some sentences and make some complex ones.

Use the Editing Checklist to edit your paragraph. <u>Underline</u> all of the subjects and circle all of the verbs in your paragraph.

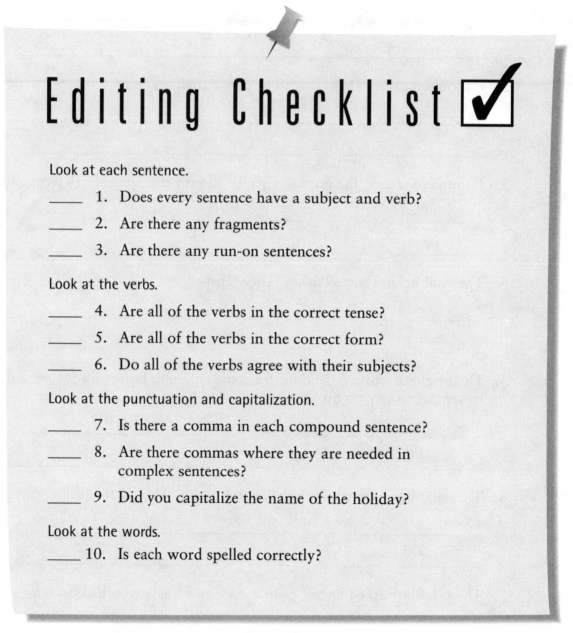

Editing Checklist ☑

Look at each sentence.

_____ 1. Does every sentence have a subject and verb?

_____ 2. Are there any fragments?

_____ 3. Are there any run-on sentences?

Look at the verbs.

_____ 4. Are all of the verbs in the correct tense?

_____ 5. Are all of the verbs in the correct form?

_____ 6. Do all of the verbs agree with their subjects?

Look at the punctuation and capitalization.

_____ 7. Is there a comma in each compound sentence?

_____ 8. Are there commas where they are needed in complex sentences?

_____ 9. Did you capitalize the name of the holiday?

Look at the words.

_____ 10. Is each word spelled correctly?

 Rewrite your paragraph in good form. To remember good form, look at page 21.

A Holiday Party!

A. The class can have a party celebrating all of the holidays in the students' paragraphs. Choose a time, either during class or outside of class, for the party.

B. Each student should bring several things related to the holiday in his or her paragraph. For example, students can bring food, traditional clothes, music, a poster, decorations, a dance to perform, a song to teach, photographs, or anything else related to the holiday. Of course, if a student brings something related to a different holiday, that is welcome too.

C. Hang the holiday paragraphs around the room.

D. Have the party and enjoy yourselves!

CHAPTER 6

Unfinished Stories

"Tell me a story," children beg. Why do children love stories so much? And is it just children? Think of all the videos that adults rent every weekend. Every movie is a story. OK, why do people love stories so much? What do you think?

In this chapter, you will try your hand at telling a story.

Picture This...

1. _____

_____

_____

2. _____

_____

_____

3. _____

_____

_____

Talk about the photograph. Then write your answers to the questions.

1. Who is telling the story?
2. What kind of story is he telling?
3. Why is he telling a story?

Here are the beginnings of three stories. You will finish one of them. Read the story beginnings and then decide which story you would like to complete.

....

1

The Lizard and the Boy

One day, Mike's mother screamed. Then she shouted, "Mike, come to the kitchen quickly! There's a lizard on the wall. You know I hate lizards in my kitchen. Kill it for me." Mike's mother ran out of the kitchen when Mike ran into it. On the wall was a small, light-brown lizard. He made a grab for it and caught it in his hand.

"Oh, Mike," said the lizard, "please don't kill me."

"Sorry," said Mike, "but my mother wants me to."

"I'm a magic lizard. I will give you three wishes if you don't kill me," said the little lizard.

"I don't believe you, but here is my first wish. I want a sports car in this kitchen right now." Mike looked at the lizard, who closed his eyes tightly.

Nothing happened.

Mike said, "I knew you weren't a magic lizard. Now I have to obey my mother's wish and kill you."

"Oh, please, no!" cried the lizard. "It's true that I am not magic, but if you save my life now, I will save yours some day."

Mike laughed, but he took the lizard outside and let him go. Mike didn't believe that the lizard could save his life, but one day, the lizard did.

This is how it happened.

....

2

One Dark Night

"Good night! It was a great party!" I waved to my friend who was standing at the front door and started walking down the road to my house. I live a little way out of town, but I had often walked home from my friend's house.

It was dark, very dark. There was no moon in the sky. It was a little chilly too, and soon, to my dismay, it started to rain. As I walked, a strong wind blew buckets of rain into my face. I was cold, wet, and miserable.

"If only I could find a place to wait until the rain stops," I thought. Luckily, in a few minutes, I saw a place. It was a small shed, and its door was banging open in the wind. I stepped inside, out of the wind and rain, and immediately felt better. I wasn't happy for long, though, because something—or was it someone?—was in the shed with me.

3

Mystery in the Dark

Laura closed her book, stood up, and stretched. It was ten o'clock, and she had been studying in the library for three hours. It was time to go to the dorm and relax. While she walked across the dark campus to her dormitory, she thought about a hot bath and some good music.

When she arrived at her floor of the dorm, everything was quiet. No one was in the hallway. "That's funny," she thought. "Where is everybody?" She unlocked the door to her room and opened it. She expected to see Kim, her roommate, but the room was dark. She reached to her right to turn on the lamp on her desk, but her hand only brushed the air. The lamp was gone. "That's strange," she thought. She turned to the left and dropped her books on the chair that was always by the door. Only this time, she heard her books fall on the floor. The chair wasn't there either. Now seriously worried, Laura reached for the light switch on the wall to her left. When the light came on, she gasped!

GET IDEAS

A. Decide which story you would like to finish. If you do not like any of the story beginnings, you may write your own story.

B. Get in a group with other students who want to finish the same story.

C. Talk about possible endings for the story. Write down ideas and helpful vocabulary as you talk. Keep in mind, however, that you will write your own story, not one group story. Your ending should be different from the other students in the group.

ORGANIZE YOUR IDEAS

A. Read over the list of ideas and words that you made when your group was talking. Think more about how you want to end the story. Add more ideas and words to your list.

B. When you tell a story, you need to organize your ideas by time. Look at your list. Put a *1* next to the first thing that will happen in your story. Put a *2* next to the second thing that will happen, and so on.

WRITE

Now write your ending to the story that you chose.

REVISE

A. Get into small groups.

B. Your teacher will collect all of the papers, and then give each group some papers written by students not in that group.

C. Each person in the group will read all of the papers. For *each* paper, follow these directions.

    1. What do you like about the story? Put a star (★) next to a word, sentence or part that you like.

    2. If you do not understand a sentence, put a question mark (?) next to that sentence.

    3. At the bottom of the paper, write one question about the story. Ask about something in the story that you want to know more about. You can also ask about something that is not clear to you. **You must write one question on each paper.** Do not ask a question about grammar.

D. After all the groups are finished, you will get back your paper. If there are any question marks on it, think of a way to write those sentences more clearly. Ask your teacher or another student if you need help. Then, answer the questions on the bottom of your paper.

Look at the questions your classmates wrote on your paper. Will your story be better if you add the answers? You are the writer, so you can decide to include the answers or not.

REVISION REVIEW

Read the following student paragraph. Think about the things you have learned and answer these questions with your class.

1. What do you like about this paragraph?
2. Is the paragraph about one main idea?
3. Is there a good topic sentence?
4. Are all of the supporting sentences relevant to the main idea?
5. Are the supporting sentences in a good order?
6. Did the writer use enough transitions?
7. Did the writer give enough details?
8. Does the paragraph have a good conclusion?

> ### Imminent Danger
>
> Mike was walking down the road. It had rained the night before and the road was wet. He was going to meet a friend. While he was walking, he heard a small voice call him. He stopped and looked all around, but he couldn't find where the voice was coming from. He started to walk again. After a little while, he heard the same voice again. The voice came from near his feet. He saw a small hole. In the hole was the lizard. The lizard called to him. Mike bent down to hear the lizard's voice. When he bent down, a shot passed over his head. The lizard said to him, "I saved your life!" The lizard saved his life in the end.

E. Look at your own paper and ask yourself the questions in the Revision Review. Do you need to make any more changes?

 Rewrite your story.

EDIT

Here are a few problem sentences taken from one story ending. Why are they a problem?

One Dark Night

1. Because I was so happy to be out of the rain.

2. After I had stood by the door for a few minutes.

3. Although I was terrified.

4. When I turned on my flashlight.

5. Before I could run.

Complex Sentence Problem: Fragments

These sentences are a problem for the reader because they do not give enough information. They are incomplete, and leave the reader with questions.

1. Because I was so happy to be out of the rain. (*What happened?*)
2. After I had stood by the door for a few minutes. (*What happened next?*)
3. Although I was terrified. (*What did the writer do?*)
4. When I turned on my flashlight. (*What did he or she see ?*)
5. Before I could run. (*What did the something or someone in the shed do?*)

Each of these sentences is made of one dependent clause. We know that they are dependent because each one _____ with a subordinate conjunction. When a dependent clause stands by itself as a sentence, it gives incomplete information. As we learned in previous chapters, an incomplete sentence is called a **fragment.** If you write a dependent clause as a separate sentence, it is a fragment.

Exercise 1

Look at one student's story ending. Write *F* above the fragments and *G* above the good sentences.

Mystery in the Dark

1. _____   2. _____   3. _____

Laura gasped because her room was a mess! Then, she fainted. When she

4. _____   5. _____

woke up. She started to put her things in their right places. After she finished

6. _____

cleaning up her room, she still couldn't find her desk anywhere. Just then,

7. _____   8. _____

the girl in the next room came to Laura's room. She had lost her bed. While

9. _____

another friend had lost a lamp. It was very strange because every person in

10. _____   11. _____

the dorm had lost one thing. This dorm had one empty room. Everybody

---

went there because they wondered about what had happened in that room.

12. ____   13. ____   14. ____

When they opened the door. They were surprised. There were all the lost

15. ____   16. ____

things! Since the students were very nervous. They grabbed their stuff and

17. ____

quickly left. After that, nothing like this ever happened in that dorm again.

18. ____

It is still a mystery.

Ways to Fix a Fragment

Every dependent clause must be joined to an independent clause. This makes a complex sentence. To fix a fragment, add an independent clause to the dependent clause, or join the dependent clause to an independent clause before or after it in the sentence.

Fragment: *When she woke up.*
Sentence: *When she woke up, she started to put her things in their right places.*
Fragment: *While another friend had lost her lamp.*
Sentence: *She had lost her bed while another friend had lost her lamp.*

Exercise 2

Look at Exercise 1 again and correct any fragments by joining the fragments to sentences before or after them. Remember to use the correct punctuation for complex sentences.

Exercise 3

Add an independent clause to each of these dependent clauses.

One Dark Night

1. Because I was so happy to be out of the rain, _____

    _____

2. After I stood by the door for a few minutes, _____

    _____

3. Although I was terrified, _____

_____

4. When I turned on my flashlight, _____

_____

5. Before I could run, _____

_____

Use the Editing Checklist to check your own paper for fragments and other problems.

Editing Checklist ✔

Underline all of the subjects and verbs in your paragraph.
Look at each sentence.

_____ 1. Does every sentence have a subject and verb?

_____ 2. Are there any fragments?

_____ 3. Are there any run-on sentences?

Look at the verbs.

_____ 4. Are all of the verbs in the correct tense?

_____ 5. Are all of the verbs in the correct form?

_____ 6. Do all of the verbs agree with their subjects?

Look at the punctuation and capitalization.

_____ 7. Is there a comma after each transition?

_____ 8. Is there a comma in each compound sentence?

_____ 9. Are there commas where they are needed
           in complex sentences?

Look at the words.

_____ 10. Is each word spelled correctly?

Rewrite your paragraph in good form. To remember good form, look at page 21.

A Play

A. Form three groups, one group for each story. Students should join the group of the story they finished. If anyone wrote their own story, he or she can work alone or join one of the groups.

B. Each student in the group should read all of the story endings of the group. Then, the students should choose one of the endings to dramatize.

C. The members of the group should write a play dramatizing the whole story—the beginning and the ending they chose.

D. The students will perform the plays in class. If a video camera is available, they can be recorded and played back.

CHAPTER **7**

A Favorite Place

You probably have a favorite place, a place you love to be. Maybe you feel safe, secure, and peaceful in your favorite place. Maybe it's an exciting place where you feel very much alive. Your favorite place may be beautiful or only ordinary-looking. It might be a room, a park, a city street, a secret place in the woods, a beach, or a club. What is your favorite place? Only you know.

Picture This...

1. _____

_____

_____

2. _____

_____

_____

3. _____

_____

_____

Talk about the photograph. Then write your answers to the questions.

1. Where is this place?
2. What does it look like?
3. How does this place make you feel?

GET IDEAS

To get ideas about your favorite place, draw a picture of it below. It does not have to be a beautiful picture. Try to put in as much detail as possible. If you do not want to draw a picture, you can make a word picture of the place. To make a word picture, write the names of objects on the paper in the same place that they would be if you were drawing a picture.

Also, brainstorm about the following questions. Look again at the photo page for ideas.

1. Why do you like this place?

2. What do you do there?

3. Write some words that tell how you feel in this place.

ORGANIZE YOUR IDEAS

A. When you write about *space,* you need to organize your ideas differently than when you write about *time.* When you write about space, you need to arrange the details in a clear way. The readers must be able to see the place in their minds as they read. Compare these two descriptions. Which one is easier to picture in your mind? Discuss the reasons why.

Paragraph A

My favorite place is my bedroom because I can do anything I like there. My bed is under the window, so I can hear the birds in the morning. My desk is next to the door, but I rarely study there. Usually I sit on my bed to study. I have a beautiful, old chest of drawers with my jewelry box and bottles of perfume on it. Also, there is a fat, comfortable chair in my room. Sometimes I sit there to read, and sometimes I just throw my clothes on it. I love to listen to music in my room too. I have a stereo. It is on a bookcase. Also, there is a mirror above the chest of drawers. Sometimes I stand in front of it and pretend that I am a singer in a rock band. Also, there is a basket for my cat to sleep in next to the bookcase. Finally, there is a nightstand next to my bed. It holds my clock radio, a few empty Diet Pepsi cans, and several empty plates with crumbs on them.

Paragraph B

My favorite place is my bedroom because I can do anything I like there. When you come into my room, my desk is on the right, next to the wall. It is completely covered with papers and books, so I rarely study there. In the corner is a fat, comfortable chair. Sometimes I sit there to read, and sometimes I just throw my clothes on it. In the middle of the next wall is a window, and my bed is under it. I love listening to the birds in the morning when I am still half asleep. Also, I usually study on my bed since my desk is such a mess. There is a nightstand to the right of the bed. It holds my clock radio, a few empty Diet Pepsi cans, and several empty plates with crumbs on them. In the middle of the next wall is a low bookcase with three shelves. My stereo is on the bookcase, and I love to listen to music when I am in my room. On the floor to the left of the bookcase is a basket for my cat to sleep in. Next to the basket is the door to my closet. In the middle of the wall across from my bed is a beautiful old chest of drawers with my jewelry box and bottles of perfume on it. There is a mirror above the chest. Sometimes I stand in front of it and pretend that I am a singer in a rock band. My room isn't very big, but I enjoy being in it very much.

Now draw a picture of this bedroom below.

B. Look back at the picture you drew of your favorite place. Circle the spot in the picture or word in the word picture where you will begin your description. If you like, draw arrows to show the direction in which your paragraph will go.

WRITE

Now you are ready to write a paragraph about your own favorite place. Use the picture or word picture that you drew above. Remember to describe what you do and how you feel in this place, not just the things there. Also remember that readers should be able to see your place in their minds while they read your paragraph.

REVISE

A. Exchange your paper with a partner. Read your partner's paragraph. Follow these directions on another piece of paper.

1. Draw a picture of your partner's favorite place.
2. Put an ✗ at the starting place of the description.
3. Draw arrows to show the direction in which the description goes.

B. Get your paper back. Was your partner able to draw a clear picture from your paragraph? If not, talk to your partner and find out what was not clear in your description.

Read the following paragraph. Think about the things you have learned, and answer these questions with your class.

1. What do you like about this paragraph?
2. Is the paragraph about one main idea?
3. Is there a good topic sentence?
4. Are all of the supporting sentences relevant to the main idea?
5. Are the supporting sentences in a good order?
6. Did the writer use enough transitions?
7. Did the writer give enough details?
8. Does the paragraph have a good conclusion?
9. Is the place description organized clearly? Can you picture the place in your mind?

This student chose a very large place to describe. It is impossible to picture all of this place in your mind, so the description is a little different than for a small place. How well does the writer help you see and feel the desert?

The Desert

I love the desert because it makes me feel spiritual. I especially like the sunrise and sunset in the desert. In my country, Saudi Arabia, I go to the desert on the weekend to relax. I leave my city, Riyadh, and drive to the desert alone. Then, when I arrive at the desert in the evening, I walk. I listen to the birds in the bushes and small trees. I look at the tall sand dunes, and I look far away to the hills. In the desert, there is so much space. I can see for 40 kilometers. I look at everything around me, especially the orange and red sunset. When the night comes, I feel relaxed. Then, I look at the sky and the stars in the sky. I can't forget the beautiful sky. Finally, I feel happy, and I feel close to God with that beautiful picture. I lay my blankets on the sand, build a fire and eat some dinner. I make Arabian coffee. Then, I go to bed because I am waiting for another beautiful picture in the morning. I mean the sunrise.

C. Look at your own paper and ask yourself the questions in the Revision Review. Do you need to make any more changes?

 Rewrite your paragraph. Revise it to make your description clearer.

EDIT

A. When you write about space, you need to use the correct words and phrases to describe where things are. These words and phrases are called **prepositions** and **prepositional phrases.**

Exercise 1

Look at the picture and fill in the description of the picture with the correct prepositions and prepositional phrases from the box on the next page.

on	above	behind	to the right of
in	below	in front of	to the left of
over	beside	next to	in the middle of
under	between	across from	in the corner

The Kitchen

This is a picture of Sherry and Tom's kitchen. (1) The kitchen table is

_____ Tom. (2) Sherry is sitting _____ a chair

with her breakfast _____ her. (3) The toaster is

_____ her. (4) In the place setting next to her, the napkin is

_____ the fork, and the plate is _____ the fork

and the knife. (5) The garbage can is _____ Sherry. (6) Tom placed

it _____ the kitchen so that it would be easy to reach. Tom is

making his breakfast at the stove. (7) The oven is _____ the broiler.

Tom is making tea in the teapot. (8) It is _____ . (9) Several

mugs are hanging _____ the sink, and the dish drainer is

_____ the sink. (10) There are some plates _____ the dish

drainer. (11) A teapot is standing _____ it. (12) There is a mixer

_____ the refrigerator. (13) The refrigerator is

_____ the freezer.

Exercise 2

Write sentences about the picture using the objects given.

the kettle / the stove <u>The kettle is on the stove.</u>

1. the mixer / the spoon / the refrigerator

   _____

2. two drawers / the dish drainer

_____

3. the cabinets / the counter

_____

4. Tom's breakfast / the skillet

_____

5. the chair / the stove

_____

6. the electrical outlet

_____

7. the saucepan / Tom

_____

8. the cat / the chair

_____

9. the blender / the mixer

_____

10. the teapot / the dish drainer

_____

B. 1. Now check your paper for prepositions and prepositional phrases. Have you used them correctly? Change or add to your paper where necessary.

2. Exchange your paper with a different partner. Draw your partner's favorite place.

3. Get your paper back. Was your partner able to draw a clear picture from your paragraph? If not, talk to your partner and find out what was not clear in your description. Make any changes that you need to so that the reader can picture your place clearly.

Use the Editing Checklist to edit your paragraph.

Editing Checklist

Underline all of the subjects and circle all of the verbs in your paragraph.

Look at each sentence.

_____ 1. Are there any fragments?

_____ 2. Are there any run-on sentences?

Look at the verbs.

_____ 3. Are all of the verbs in the correct tense?

_____ 4. Are all of the verbs in the correct form?

_____ 5. Do all of the verbs agree with their subjects?

Look at the punctuation and capitalization.

_____ 6. Do all of your sentences end with the correct punctuation?

_____ 7. Is there a comma after each transition?

_____ 8. Is there a comma in each compound sentence?

_____ 9. Are there commas where they are needed in complex sentences?

_____ 10. Does each sentence begin with a capital letter?

Look at the words.

_____ 11. Did you use the correct prepositions?

_____ 12. Is each word spelled correctly?

Rewrite your paragraph in good form. To remember good form, look at page 21.

A Tourist Brochure

A. You will make a tourist brochure. The brochure will invite tourists to visit your favorite place.

B. Think of the good things about your favorite place. Why do you like to go there? Why will other people want to go there? What can someone see or do there?

C. Design and make your brochure. You can use, for example, stiff paper, tagboard, magazine pictures, your own drawing and lettering, and so on to create the brochure.

D. The brochures should be shown in the classroom next to your paragraph so that everyone in the class can enjoy them.

CHAPTER 8

The Ideal Spouse

Are you married or single? If you are single, do you ever think about getting married? Maybe you think, "Married! That's a long way in the future." Or maybe you would like to marry soon. If you are already married, you probably have a story to tell about how you met your spouse.

Have you ever thought about the person you would like to marry? Most people would say, "Yes, I want to marry someone good-looking and rich!" But what about the inside of that person, his or her character? Most people agree that a spouse's character is the most important thing for a happy marriage.

In this chapter, you will imagine and write about your ideal spouse. If you are already married, you can write about your real spouse.

Picture This...

1. _____

_____

_____

2. _____

_____

_____

3. _____

_____

_____

Talk about the photo. Then write your answers to the questions.

1. How can you describe each person?
2. What are they feeling?
3. How do you feel when you look at the photo?

GET IDEAS

Look at this chart of adjectives. Each adjective is a *quality*. A person's character is made of many qualities. Do you know what all of these words mean? Talk about them. Then, choose four qualities to describe your ideal or real spouse.

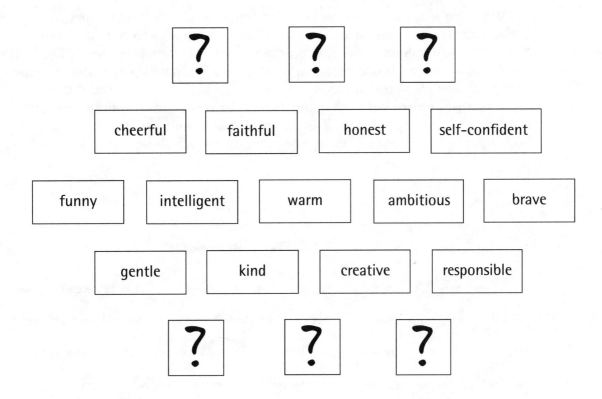

To get ideas about your spouse, you will try something new. It is called **freewriting.** Freewriting works like this. Your teacher will give you some time, about five or ten minutes. In that time, you will write as much as you can about your spouse *without stopping*. Write in connected sentences, not in words or phrases as you do in brainstorming or webbing. However, do not worry about grammar, spelling, or good paragraph form. Also, you may write a word in your own language if you do not know it in English, but try not to do this very often.

The purpose of freewriting is not to write a good paragraph, but to get a lot of ideas from your head onto the paper. Thus, you must keep writing for the whole time that the teacher gives you. Do not stop writing, and do not erase. Scratch out anything you do not want. If you cannot think of anything to say, write the same word again and again, or write "I don't know." Soon, you will have a new idea.

As you write, remember to write down as many ideas as possible. Do not worry about grammar, and **do not stop!**

Before you begin, look back at the photo page for ideas.

Now, freewrite about your ideal or real spouse. Write about the qualities you have chosen. Why do you think they are important in a husband or wife?

After you finish freewriting, read what you have written. <u>Underline</u> any ideas that you want to use in your paragraph. You can add any new ideas that you think of.

ORGANIZE YOUR IDEAS

A. Read your freewriting. Which quality is the most important to you? Which is the least important? To show that in your writing, you need to write about them in order of importance.

Writing about ideas in order of importance is one way to organize ideas by *logic*. When you write about something that happened, you organize your writing by time. When you write about a place, you organize your writing by space. When you write about ideas, you must organize your ideas *logically*, in a way that makes sense to the reader. If your ideas are all mixed up, the reader will not understand them.

When you write about the qualities of your real or ideal spouse, you can organize them from most important to least important or from least important to most important. Read these two paragraphs and decide which way you think is best.

Paragraph A

> ### Choosing a Husband
>
> I am only 20 years old now, and I am enjoying life as a student. I don't think about marriage very often. But I am sure that someday I will get married. When I get married, I hope that my husband will have these qualities. First, the man that I want to marry will be intelligent. Intelligent men are more interesting to me than dull men. I don't want to be bored by my husband. Secondly, it is important for him to be a kind man. I want him to be kind and helpful both to me and to other people. A kind man will care about me and try to make my life better. Life is easier and more enjoyable when you have a kind spouse. Next, I want my husband to be honest. If he is honest, I can always believe him, and our communication will be better. If a man is dishonest or keeps secrets from me, I will always be unsure of his love and worried about our marriage. Most of all, I want a faithful husband. I need to trust that he will always stay close to me with his body and, more importantly, his heart. A good marriage needs complete trust, and for that, I need a faithful husband. If my real husband has all the qualities of my ideal husband, we will have a wonderful marriage.

Circle the words in Paragraph A that show the order. This paragraph is organized from most / least important to least/ most important.

Paragraph B

Choosing a Husband

I am only 20 years old now, and I am enjoying my life as a student. I don't think about marriage very often. But I am sure that someday I will get married. When I get married, I hope that my husband will have these qualities. Most importantly, I want a faithful husband. I need to trust that he will always stay close to me with his body and, more importantly, his heart. A good marriage needs complete trust, and for that, I need a faithful husband. Also, I want my husband to be honest. If he is honest, I can always believe him, and our communication will be better. If a man is dishonest or keeps secrets from me, I will always be unsure of his love and worried about our marriage. In addition, it is important for him to be a kind man. I want him to be kind and helpful both to me and to other people. A kind man will care about me and try to make my life better. Life is easier and more enjoyable when you have a kind spouse. Finally, the man that I want to marry will be intelligent because intelligent men are more interesting to me than dull men. I don't want to be bored by my husband. If my real husband has all the qualities of my ideal husband, we will have a wonderful marriage.

Circle the words that show the order of Paragraph B. This paragraph is organized from most/ least important to least/most important.

B. Which order do you prefer, A or B? Why? Make a list of the four qualities that you have chosen, and put them in the order in which you want to write about them.

most/least important   1. _____

2. _____

3. _____

least/most important   4. _____

WRITE

Write a paragraph describing the character of your ideal spouse. Explain why you chose each quality.

REVISE

In this paragraph, you have written about four qualities in order of importance. Of course, you cannot use numbers to list these four qualities. Instead, you must use transition words and phrases. These transitions show when the writer is going to introduce a new quality. How are they punctuated?

First,	Thirdly,	Moreover,	Most of all,
First of all,	Also,	Next,	Most importantly,
Secondly,	In addition,	Finally,	

Look at Paragraphs A and B again. Find and underline the transitions in both. What transitions are used in the first paragraph? In the second? Which transitions are used to show the quality of greatest importance?

Exercise 1

Read the paragraph on the next page. Decide how the writer organized the qualities of his future wife. Then, decide where the paragraph needs transitions. Write the number of the sentence and the transition word in the chart under the paragraph.

My Future Wife

(1) When I close my eyes, I can see my future wife. (2) She will be beautiful, of course! (3) But she will be beautiful on the inside also. (4) She will be a cheerful person. (5) I am a pessimist, so I want a wife to smile at me and make me happy. (6) I like to hear laughter in the house. (7) I want a self-confident wife. (8) If she has confidence in herself, she will not be afraid to try new things, and she will succeed. (9) If she fails, she will not be afraid to try again. (10) She will be gentle. (11) When I have a hard day at work, I want to come home to a gentle wife. (12) Her soft way will make me feel better. (13) I think children need a gentle mother. (14) My wife will always be faithful to me. (15) I want her to love only me and not look at any other man. (16) Then, our hearts will be safe.

This paragraph is organized from most/ least important to least/most important.

NUMBER OF THE SENTENCE   TRANSITIONS

————   ——————————————
————   ——————————————
————   ——————————————
————   ——————————————
————   ——————————————
————   ——————————————

A. Exchange your paper with a partner. Read your partner's paragraph. Then, answer these questions about it.

1. What do you like about your partner's paper? Put a star (★) next to a word, sentence, or idea that you like.

2. In the spaces below, list the qualities your partner wants in a spouse. Did your partner organize the qualities from most important to least important or from least important to most important?

most/least important   1. _____

                              2. _____

                              3. _____

least/most important   4. _____

3. How did you know which was the most important quality?
4. Does a transition introduce each quality?

B. Get your paper back from your partner and talk to him or her about your paper. Was your organization clear so that your partner could understand it?

REVISION REVIEW

Read the following student paragraph. Think about the things you have learned, and answer these questions with your class.

1. What do you like about this paragraph?
2. Is the paragraph about one main idea?
3. Is there a good topic sentence?
4. Are all of the supporting sentences relevant to the main idea?
5. Are the supporting sentences in a good order?
6. Did the writer use enough transitions?
7. Did the writer give enough details?
8. Does the paragraph have a good conclusion?

A Good Life Partner

My husband is a very good man. First of all, he is loving. He loves animals, flowers, and people. He has a lot of flowers and pictures of animals at our home. He especially loves wolves and whales. Also, he is very energetic, so he goes to play tennis, to scuba dive, and to play basketball. He likes to swim in the sea too, but he can't swim here because we are far away from the beach. He is very careful while driving. He likes to shop, so we often go to the mall. He is very happy when he buys new things. Finally, he is very helpful. He usually helps me with the housework. Sometimes he cooks, and sometimes he washes our clothes. He is a very good life partner, so I love him very much.

C. Look at your own paper and ask yourself the questions in the Revision Review. Do you need to make any more changes?

 Rewrite your paragraph so that its meaning is clearer.

EDIT

You have learned about three kinds of sentences: simple, compound, and complex. Which is the *best* kind of sentence to use in your writing? Read the three drafts of a paragraph below and circle the kind of sentence used in each draft. Then, decide which is the best kind of sentence to use.

Draft A

Ernest

Ernest is my wonderful husband. He always talks with a smile. His smile makes me laugh all the time. He is a very funny and carefree person. We have free time sometimes. Then, we play like children. He is also a responsible person. He is a good man. He cares for me and our house. He always pays the bills and accounts.

SIMPLE—COMPOUND—COMPLEX

Draft B

I love Ernest very much because he is a wonderful husband. Since he is a happy person, he always talks with a smile. When he smiles, I laugh. We play together like children when we have free time because he is a funny and carefree person. Because he is a responsible person, I think that he is a good man. Because he cares for me and our house, he always pays the bills and accounts.

SIMPLE—COMPOUND—COMPLEX

Draft C

> *Ernest is a wonderful husband, so I love him very much. He always talks with a smile, and his smile makes me laugh all the time. He is very funny, and he is a carefree person. We have free time sometimes, and then we play like children. He is also a responsible person, and he is a good man. He cares for me and our house, so he always pays the bills and accounts.*
>
> SIMPLE—COMPOUND—COMPLEX

Which kind of sentence do you think is the best to use in your writing? Actually, that is a trick question. There is *no* best kind of sentence. Good writing uses a mix of all three.

" Variety is the spice of life."
ENGLISH PROVERB

What do you think this proverb means? Think of a song. A good song is not the same all the way through. Sometimes it is fast; sometimes it is slow. Sometimes it is loud; sometimes it is soft. Good writing is the same. A paragraph is more interesting to read when several kinds of sentences are used.

It is usually boring when every sentence begins with the subject of the sentence. If you sometimes start your sentences with transitions (*then, secondly, after that,* etc.) or prepositional phrases (*at night, before class, in the corner,* etc.), you will make your sentences more interesting.

Read the fourth draft of the paragraph about Ernest. Now there is a variety of sentences and transitions. Do you agree that this draft is more enjoyable to read?

Draft D

> *Ernest is my wonderful husband. He always talks with a smile, and his smile makes me laugh all the time. In fact, he is a very funny and carefree person. When we have free time, we play together like children. Also, Ernest is a responsible person and a good man. Because he cares for me and our house, he always pays the bills and accounts.*

Exercise 1

Rewrite each group of sentences. Combine them or separate them to make different kinds of sentences. Add transitions and move prepositional phrases to vary the sentences. The first one has been done for you.

> I am a night person. I want to marry another night person. I hate cheerfulness in the morning!

> *I want to marry a night person because I am a night person. I hate*

> *cheerfulness in the morning!*

1. I don't like to talk in the morning. I don't have enough energy to be pleasant. I want to be grumpy and silent.

   _____

   _____

2. I shouldn't marry a morning person. If my wife chatters and chirps in the morning, I will go crazy.

   _____

   _____

3. I need to marry a night person. Another night person will frown at me in the morning. She'll leave me alone. She will understand me.

   _____

   _____

A. Look at the sentences that you wrote about one of the qualities of your ideal spouse. On another piece of paper, rewrite them two times. Each time, change the sentences in some way. You can join some of the sentences or make longer sentences into shorter ones. You can also add transitions or prepositional phrases at the beginning of some of the sentences. Which of your three drafts do you like the best? Why?

B. Make changes in some other sentences in your paragraph to make them more interesting.

C. Use the Editing Checklist to continue editing your paragraph. It is on the next page.

Editing Checklist ☑

Underline all of the subjects and circle all of the verbs in your paragraph.

Look at each sentence.

_____ 1. Are there any fragments?

_____ 2. Are there any run-on sentences?

_____ 3. Is there a variety of sentences?

Look at the verbs.

_____ 4. Are all of the verbs in the correct tense?

_____ 5. Are all of the verbs in the correct form?

_____ 6. Do all of the verbs agree with their subjects?

Look at the punctuation and capitalization.

_____ 7. Do all of the sentences end with the correct punctuation?

_____ 8. Is there a comma after each transition?

_____ 9. Is there a comma in each compound sentence?

_____ 10. Are there commas where they are needed in complex sentences?

_____ 11. Does each sentence begin with a capital letter?

Look at the words.

_____ 12. Were the correct prepositions used?

_____ 13. Is each word spelled correctly?

 Rewrite your paragraph in good form. To remember good form, look at page 21.

A Pen Pal

A. Imagine that you will join a pen pal club. You must write a letter describing the kind of person you want to write to. However, in this letter, you will ask for a pen pal who shares similar interests, activities, and ideas, not one with certain qualities. For example, you may request to write to a pen pal who is interested in hiking, rock music, and zero population growth.

B. In this letter, you will also give a very short description of yourself.

C. If anyone in the class is really interested in writing to a pen pal, your teacher can get information about various pen pal clubs, both through the traditional mail and e-mail.

CHAPTER 9

What's Your Opinion?

You are sitting around with your friends after class, having a soda and eating a snack. Someone brings up a controversial subject, and soon everyone is part of a heated discussion. Some people raise their voices, and some even get angry. Everyone wants to express an opinion.

Has this ever happened to you? Most people have some strong opinions and enjoy discussing them.

What is your opinion?   Here are some opinions for you to think about and discuss with your classmates. Read these opinions and check (✔) whether you agree or disagree with them.

AGREE   DISAGREE   OPINIONS

_____   _____   1. I believe that ghosts exist.

_____   _____   2. Women should serve in the military

_____   _____   3. It is a bad idea for people to live together before they get married.

_____   _____   4. Baseball is a more interesting sport than soccer.

_____   _____   5. Space exploration is necessary.

_____   _____   6. It is OK for women with small children to work outside of the home.

_____   _____   7. UFOs have visited our planet.

_____   _____   8. Life in our world is getting worse.

Discuss your opinions with the class.

GET IDEAS

A. Choose one opinion to write about, either from the ones above or another opinion that you feel strongly about.

B. To get ideas about your opinion, try freewriting, as you did in Chapter 8. Remember to write as much as you can *without stopping*. While you write, think about your reasons for holding your opinion. Are they good reasons? What information do you have to support your reasons? Write down as many ideas as you can.

After you finish freewriting, read what you have written. If you think of any new ideas, add them to your freewriting.

ORGANIZE YOUR IDEAS

A. You have an opinion. To explain that opinion to your readers, you need to give your reasons. Reread your freewriting and underline all of the reasons for your opinion.

If you feel strongly about your opinion, you will have a lot to say about it, and you will need more than one paragraph in which to say it. For the first eight chapters of this book, you wrote papers of a single paragraph. Your writing has probably improved, and you are now ready to write longer papers.

For the last two chapters of the book, you will write papers of several paragraphs. A paper of several paragraphs is called a **composition.** In a composition, you are able to give more details and explain your ideas more completely. A composition still has a topic sentence in the first paragraph and a conclusion in the last paragraph.

B. How can you organize your ideas in a composition to help a reader understand your thinking? To help you think about this, read the following opinion paper and look at the way the ideas are organized.

Television: Not a Bad Idea

Although some parents don't allow their children to watch television, I believe that television can be good for children. First of all, television is inexpensive entertainment. On rainy Saturday afternoons, when children are driving their parents crazy, the TV can bring them some harmless fun. Also, when it is too expensive to take the whole family to a movie, the family can sit in their living room with bowls of homemade popcorn and watch a movie on television.

Secondly, television can be a good teacher. For example, small children can learn many things, such as the alphabet and numbers, on children's programs. Studies show that these programs help children do well in school. In addition, nature programs teach them about our earth and how to care for it. Parents can also use television dramas as a way to start conversations with their children about important ideas.

Most importantly, television lets children see a bigger picture of the world than their own small neighborhood. Our family cannot travel all over the globe, so the news shows them views of other people and places. The television also brings other cultures into our home through special children's programs. I want my children to see our diverse world. In conclusion, although some parents are throwing out their televisions, our family is keeping ours.

Exercise 1

Discuss the following questions about the writer's opinion with your class.

1. What is the writer's opinion? How do you know it is an opinion?

2. In what sentence do you find the opinion?

3. How many reasons does the writer give for the opinion? What are they?

4. Where do you find the most important reason?

5. Why is it necessary to support an opinion with reasons?

6. What facts or examples does the writer use to support each reason?

7. Why is it necessary to support reasons with facts or examples?

8. What kind of sentence comes at the end of the composition? What does it do?

Exercise 2

Read the following composition and fill in the outline on the next page. An *outline* is like the skeleton of the composition's ideas. Use only words or phrases.

Cats Are Best

To all of my friends with small, yappy dogs or large, leaping dogs, I have one thing to say. Cats make the best pets. First, cats can take care of themselves. While a dog needs its owner to give it baths, a cat is quite happy to give itself baths, thank you. Also, a dog's owner must take it for a walk every day in all kinds of weather. A cat prefers to walk alone, or better yet, to stay inside and curl up in a warm armchair.

Next, cats are cheap. Dogs need large amounts of expensive food. A dog owner needs a second job just to feed his dog. Cats, on the other hand, are happy with a handful of dried food. Also, when dog owners go away on vacation, they must spend a lot of money on a kennel. However, cats only need a neighbor to check up on them from time to time.

In addition, cats have more character. A dog will love anybody; all you have to do is feed it. You have to earn a cat's respect, however. A cat will not be just anybody's friend. Dogs depend on others for their happiness too. A dog left on its own is a sad sight, while cats are quite happy with their own company. For all these reasons, my pet is a large, black cat named Marco.

Outline of "Cats Are Best"

Opinion:

Reason 1:

Support:

Reason 2:

Support:

Reason 3:

Support:

Conclusion:

C. Now make an outline for your composition. Space is given here for three reasons, but you might have a different number of reasons. Look at your freewriting to find words and phrases to use.

Composition Outline

Opinion:

Reason 1:

Support :

Reason 2:

Support:

Reason 3:

Support:

Conclusion:

WRITE

You are ready to write your first composition. You will need one paragraph for each reason that supports your opinion. Try to explain your thinking clearly so that the reader can understand why you hold your opinion.

REVISE

A. Exchange your paper with a partner. Outline your partner's paper below.

My Partner's Paper

Opinion:

Reason 1:

Support :

Reason 2:

Support:

Reason 3:

Support:

Conclusion:

Answer these questions in writing about your partner's paper.

1. What is your partner's opinion?

_____

_____

2. Did the writer give enough reasons for you?

_____

_____

3. Do all of the reasons support the opinion?

_____

_____

4. Is each reason supported by facts or examples?

_____

_____

5. Does the composition need any more transition words or phrases?

_____

_____

6. Is there anything you do not understand?

_____

_____

7. Did the writer make a good argument for his or her opinion?

_____

_____

B. Get your paper back from your partner. Talk to your partner about the outline of your paragraph.

Rewrite your paper. Change and add anything that you need to.

EDIT

As a class, make up the Editing Checklist, and use it to check your own paper. *Do not look back at previous chapters!*

Editing Checklist ✔

Look at each sentence.

Look at the verbs.

Look at the punctuation and capitalization.

Look at the words.

 Rewrite your paragraph in good form. To remember good form, look at page 21.

 **A Step Further...**

Letters to the Editor

A. Read all of the other students' papers. For this activity, imagine that these papers are newspaper editorials. Take notes while you read of things you do not agree with. You may not agree with an opinion, a reason for an opinion, or a fact.

B. Choose one thing you disagree with to write about. Write a letter to the editor of the newspaper. In your letter, explain (1) what you disagree with, (2) why you disagree with it, and (3) what you believe is true. Begin with "Dear Editor" and keep your letter short. Newspaper editors do not print long letters.

C. Then as a class make a newspaper. The newspaper can contain both the student opinion compositions and the letters to the editor.

CHAPTER 10

Ten Years from Now

What is today's date? Now think about that same date ten years in the future. What will your life be like then? Of course, no one can really predict the future, but it is fun to think about what the future will hold. What are your wishes, dreams, and plans for the future? How do you picture your life ten years from now? That is the picture you will write about in this chapter.

1. _____

_____

_____

2. _____

_____

_____

Talk about the photograph. Then write your answers to the questions.

1. What is happening in the photograph?
2. Do you want your life to be the same or similar in ten years?

GET IDEAS

A. In this book you have learned about a number of ways to get ideas. With your class, make a list of the different ways and discuss them. Which way works best for you? Why?

B. Choose your favorite way to get ideas and use it to gather ideas about your own future, ten years from now. If you want, you can look back at the photo page for ideas.

ORGANIZE YOUR IDEAS

A. How should you organize your paper this time—by time, space, or logic? Look at the ideas you gathered. Can you see one way or several ways to organize them? With your class, discuss all the possible ways to organize a composition about this topic.

B. On your own, decide how you will organize your ideas. Make some notes or an outline.

C. Find a partner. Explain how you will organize your composition. Listen to your partner and ask questions. If you see any problems in your partner's plan, point them out to him or her. Listen while your partner does the same for you.

WRITE

Write the first draft of your composition following your plan.

REVISE

A. As a class, review all of the things that you have learned about revising your writing. Make a list of these things.

B. Then follow these steps:

1. Get into small groups.

2. The teacher will collect all of the papers, and then give each group some papers written by people not in that group. Each paper should have a blank sheet of paper attached to it.

3. Each person in the group will read all of the papers. For *each* paper, each member of the group will make one suggestion for revising the paper. Look at the list that the class made to help you make suggestions. Write the suggestions on the blank sheet attached to each paper.

4. Each group will decide which paper in their group describes the most *interesting* future. A member of the group or your teacher will read that paper aloud for the whole class to hear.

C. Get your paper back. Read the suggestions your classmates made.

Rewrite your composition and make any revisions (changes) that will improve it.

EDIT

Congratulations! You have reached the end of the book. By now you should have learned a lot about editing your writing. In this chapter, you will rely only on yourself and a partner to edit your composition.

A. On your own, brainstorm about editing. Write down as many things as you can remember that you need to check for when you edit. Think about grammar, punctuation, capitalization, spelling, and the form of your paper. Be specific.

B. Get together with a partner. Compare your list with your partner's list. Did you forget anything? Add those things to your list.

C. Use your list to edit your composition.

Rewrite your paragraph in good form. To remember good form, look at page 21.

A Step Further...

A Day in the Life of...

A. Reread your own composition. Imagine one average day, or one perfect day, ten years in the future. On a separate piece of paper, make a schedule for that day. What will happen in the morning? Afternoon? Evening? Night?

B. In your class, form several small groups. Read the group members' compositions.

C. Each member of the group will describe their day in the future. The other members will listen and ask questions.

QUICK CHECK

An Editing Guide to Academic English

Use this guide (1) to help you check your work after you write it and (2) to help you fix your mistakes after your teacher returns your paper to you.

MARKING SYMBOLS

Your teacher might use the following symbols when marking your paper.

V = verb problem (p. 139)

S/V = subject/verb agreement (p. 144)

Frag = sentence fragment (p. 145)

RO = run-on sentence (p. 146)

WF = word form (p. 148)

WW = wrong word (p. 151)

SP = spelling (p. 155)

P = punctuation (p. 158)

C = capitalization (p. 160)

O = something missing
∧   (no information given)

Under each symbol, you will find rules. Look at these rules when you write your paragraphs.

Note: All of the rules in *Quick Check* apply to academic English. The grammar is "correct" when it is appropriate for academic English and "incorrect" when it is inappropriate for academic English.

When your teacher returns your paper to you, your errors may be marked with these symbols. What is wrong with each sentence? First, find the page in *Quick Check* that will help you find the correct answer. Write the page number in the parentheses ( ). Then write the correction on the line under the example.

1. V = verb problem

   V
   Yesterday, I eat breakfast early.

   (p.   ) _____

2. V = verb problem

   V
   They are talk together now.

   (p.   ) _____

3. S/V = subject/verb agreement

   S/V
   She get up late every day.

   (p.   ) _____

4. Frag = sentence fragment

   Frag
   We hungry in the morning.

   (p.   ) _____

5. RO = run-on sentence

   RO
   I love the night I relax then.

   (p.   ) _____

6. WF = word form

   WF
   He has three book.

   (p.   ) _____

7. WF = word form

   WF
   Jack is old than Karen.

   (p.   ) _____

8. WW = wrong word

   WW
   She went at the morning.

   (p.   ) _____

9. SP = spelling

   sp
   He fixs breakfast.

   (p.   ) _____

10. P = punctuation

    P
    You can see the stars

    (p.   ) _____

11. C = capitalization

    C   C
    at night, He goes out.

    (p.   ) _____

12. O = something missing

    ∧   O
    The sky is clean∧the morning.

    (p.   ) _____

V

Verb Problem

The verb *to talk* is used as an example.

1. Do I need to use the *simple present*?

MEANING	VERB FORM	NEGATIVE
a. a habit *I sleep late every Saturday morning.* **b.** a fact *They are brothers.*	I, you, we, they *talk* He, she, it *talks*	**to do** + **not** + verb I, you, we, they *do not talk* He, she, it *does not talk*
c. some verbs are usually used only in the simple present see love need hear like have smell hate believe taste want know feel think (opinion)	The Verb *to be*	
	I *am* You, we, they *are* He, she, it *is*	I *am not* You, we, they *are not* He, she, it *is not*

2. Do I need to use the *present progressive/continuous*?

MEANING	VERB FORM	NEGATIVE
something happening at the time of speaking *Look! It is snowing.*	**to be** + verb + **ing** I *am talking* You, we, they *are talking* he, she, it *is talking*	**to be** + verb + **ing** I *am not talking* You, we, they *are not talking* he, she, it *is not talking*

3. Do I need to use the *present perfect?*

MEANING	VERB FORM	NEGATIVE
a. happened in the past, but the time is not given *We have seen that movie.*	*to have* + past participle I, you, we, they *have talked* He, she, it *has talked*	*to have* + *not* + past participle I, you, we, they *have not talked* He, she, it *has not talked*
b. began in the past and continues to the present *Ana has been here for six months.*		

4. Do I need to use the *simple past?*

MEANING	VERB FORM	NEGATIVE
happened and finished in the past *I called her last night.*	Regular verbs: verb + *ed* I, you, he, she, it, we, they *talked* Irregular verbs: See list on page 142 for forms.	All verbs: *did* + *not* + verb I, you, he, she, it, we, they *did not talk*
	The Verb *to be*	
	I, he, she, it *was* You, we, they *were*	I, he, she, it *was not* You, we, they *were not*

5. Do I need to use the *past progressive/continuous?*

MEANING	VERB FORM	NEGATIVE
happening at a time in the past *I was studying at 10 p.m. last night.*	*to be* (past) + verb + *ing* I, he, she, it *was talking* You, we, they *were talking*	*to be* + *not* + verb + *ing* I, he, she, it *was not talking* You, we, they *were not talking*

6. Do I need to use the *past perfect?*

MEANING	VERB FORM	NEGATIVE
happened in the past before another time in the past *They had left before I arrived. Nobody was there.*	*had* + past participle I, you, he, she, it, we, they *had talked*	*had* + *not* + Past Participle I, you, he, she, it, we, they *had not talked*

7. Do I need to use the *simple future?*

MEANING	VERB FORM	NEGATIVE
something will happen in the future	**a.** *will* + verb I, you, he, she, it, we, they *will talk* **b.** *to be* + *going to* + verb I *am going to talk* You, we, they *are going to talk* He, she, it *is going to talk*	**a.** *will* + *not* + verb I, you, he, she, it, we, they *will not talk* **b.** *to be* + *going to* + *not* + verb I *am not going to talk* You, we, they *are not going to talk* He, she, it *is not going to talk*

Some Irregular Verbs

PRESENT	PAST	PAST PARTICIPLE	PRESENT	PAST	PAST PARTICIPLE
am, is, are	was, were	been	hold	held	held
beat	beat	beaten, beat	hurt	hurt	hurt
become	became	become	keep	kept	kept
begin	began	begun	know	knew	known
bend	bent	bent	leave	left	left
bet	bet	bet	let	let	let
bite	bit	bitten	lose	lost	lost
bleed	bled	bled	make	made	made
blow	blew	blown	meet	met	met
break	broke	broken	pay	paid	paid
bring	brought	brought	read	read	read
build	built	built	ride	rode	ridden
buy	bought	bought	ring	rang	rung
catch	caught	caught	run	ran	run
choose	chose	chosen	say	said	said
come	came	come	see	saw	seen
cost	cost	cost	sell	sold	sold
cut	cut	cut	send	sent	sent
dig	dug	dug	shake	shook	shaken
do	did	done	show	showed	shown
draw	drew	drawn	shut	shut	shut
drink	drank	drunk	sing	sang	sung
drive	drove	driven	sit	sat	sat
eat	ate	eaten	spend	spent	spent
fight	fought	fought	stand	stood	stood
find	found	found	steal	stole	stolen
fly	flew	flown	swim	swam	swum
forget	forgot	forgotten	take	took	taken
forgive	forgave	forgiven	teach	taught	taught
freeze	froze	frozen	tell	told	told
get	got	gotten	think	thought	thought
give	gave	given	throw	threw	thrown
go	went	gone	understand	understood	understood
have	had	had	wake	woke	woken
hear	heard	heard	wear	wore	worn
hide	hid	hidden, hid	win	won	won
hit	hit	hit	write	wrote	written

8. What do I do with *one subject and several verbs?*

---

a. When one subject has several verbs, all the verbs must be the same tense.

INCORRECT: *I went to bed and think about the day.*

CORRECT: *I went to bed and thought about the day.*

b. When one subject has several verbs, all the verbs must have the same form.

INCORRECT: *She goes outside and look at the stars.*

CORRECT: *She goes outside and looks at the stars.*

INCORRECT: *The children were running and jump.*

CORRECT: *The children were running and jumping.*

---

9. Did I use a *modal (should, can, have to,* etc.) correctly?

---

a. A modal is followed by the simple form of the verb.

INCORRECT: *My sister can swims.*

CORRECT: *My sister can swim.*

INCORRECT: *I must to study tonight.*

CORRECT: *I must study tonight.*

*The word *to* is part of some modals, such as *have to* and *ought to.*

b. To add *not* to a modal, put it between the modal and the verb.

INCORRECT: *You no should drive after you drink alcohol.*

CORRECT: *You should not drive after you drink alcohol.*

Subject/Verb Agreement

Subject/verb agreement means that the verb is the correct form in academic English for the subject. When the verb is the correct form for the subject, we say the subject and the verb "agree." When the verb is not the correct form in academic English for the subject, they do not agree.

INCORRECT: *I are here. (The subject and verb do not agree.)*
CORRECT: *I am here. (The subject and verb agree.)*

1. Do I need to *add -s* to the verb?

> Remember: *he, she,* and *it* need an *-s* at the end of the verb.
> INCORRECT: *She run to the bus.*
> CORRECT: *She runs to the bus.*

2. Is the noun *singular* or *plural?*

> Noncount nouns are singular.
> *Food* (noncount/singular) *is necessary for life.*
> *Apples* (count/plural) *are round*

3. Do I need *there is* or *there are?*

> Use *there is* when the word after it is singular. Use *there are* when the word after it is plural.
> *There is a smile* (singular) *on her face.*
> *There are smiles* (plural) *on their faces.*

4. Is it *singular* or *plural?*

Certain words are singular: *each, every, everyone, everybody*	*All* is a plural word.
Each child is special.	*All babies are beautiful.*
Every student hates homework.	
Everyone wants to be happy.	
Everybody needs food to live.	

5. Did I choose the *right word as the subject?*

> The verb must agree with the subject, and not with the words after the subject.
>
> **a.** INCORRECT: *The students on the bus is going on the trip.*
>
>   CORRECT: *The students on the bus are going on the trip.*
>   *("The students" is the subject, not "the bus.")*
>
> **b.** INCORRECT: *One of the apples are rotten.*
>
>   CORRECT: *One of the apples is rotten.*
>   *("One" is the subject, not "apples.")*

Frag

Sentence Fragment

A fragment is only part of a sentence, not a complete sentence.

1. How can I change a *simple sentence fragment?*

> A simple sentence fragment can have three problems. Here are the problems and ways to fix them.
>
> **a. No subject**
>
>   INCORRECT: *Then, went to the store together.*
>   V
>
>   CORRECT: *Then, they went to the store together.*
>   S   V
>
> **b. No verb**
>
>   INCORRECT: *Lucy and her pet lizard.*
>   S   S
>
>   CORRECT: *Lucy and her pet lizard danced in the rain.*
>   S   S   V
>
> **c. No subject or verb**
>
>   INCORRECT: *Difficult to spell English words.*
>
>   CORRECT: *It is difficult to spell English words.*
>   S V

2. How can I fix a *complex sentence fragment?*

A complex sentence fragment has a different problem. A complex sentence is made of independent and dependent clauses. A dependent clause begins with a subordinate conjunction (*although, because, since, when, before, after, while,* etc.). A dependent clause cannot be a sentence by itself. It must be joined to an independent clause. If you have a dependent clause not joined to an independent clause, it is a **fragment**.

a. INCORRECT: *When the rain began. The children went inside.*
     CORRECT: *When the rain began, the children went inside.*

b. INCORRECT: *The children went inside. When the rain began.*
     CORRECT: *The children went inside when the rain began.*

RO

Run-on Sentence

A run-on sentence is two or three sentences joined together incorrectly to make only one sentence.

1. How can I fix a *run-on simple sentence?*

A run-on simple sentence can have two problems.

a. The independent clauses are not separated at all.

                   S   S   V   S   V

     INCORRECT: *John and Paul love soccer they often play after school.*
                    INDEPENDENT CLAUSE   INDEPENDENT CLAUSE

b. The independent clauses are separated by a comma. A comma alone can never separate two independent clauses.

     INCORRECT: *John and Paul love soccer, they often play after school.*

There are three ways to fix a run-on sentence. Choose the way that is the best for your paragraph.

a. Make two sentences.

     CORRECT: *John and Paul love soccer. They often play after school.*

b. Add a coordinate conjunction.

     CORRECT: *John and Paul love soccer, **so** they often play after school.*

c. Add a subordinate conjunction.

     CORRECT: ***Because** John and Paul love soccer, they often play after school.*

2. How can I fix a *run-on compound sentence?*

A compound sentence can have another problem. Remember that a sentence usually does not have more than two independent clauses in it. If it has more than two independent clauses in it, it will probably be a run-on sentence.

Here are some examples of run-on compound sentences.

a. *Laura wanted a job, so she applied at a fast food place, and*
   INDEPENDENT CLAUSE   INDEPENDENT CLAUSE

   now she works on weekends.
   INDEPENDENT CLAUSE

b. *Laura wanted a job, she applied at a fast food place, now she works on weekends.*

c. *Laura wanted a job, so she applied at a fast food place, now she works on weekends.*

d. *Laura wanted a job she applied at a fast food place now she works on weekends.*

To fix a run-on sentence, use only two independent clauses in one sentence. Make a new sentence with any other independent clauses.

a. *Laura wanted a job, so she applied at a fast food place. Now she works on weekends.*

b. *Laura wanted a job. She applied at a fast food place, and now she works on weekends.*

1. Do I need a *noun* (or *pronoun*)?

> You need a noun (or pronoun) for three things in an English sentence.
>
> S   O   O OF A PREPOSITION
>
> *My brother gave a gift to his girlfriend.*
> <u>NOUN</u>   <u>NOUN</u>   <u>NOUN</u>
>
> **a.** You need a noun for a subject.
>
> INCORRECT: *<u>Happy</u> is important to everyone.*
>   ADJ
>
> CORRECT: *<u>Happiness</u> is important to everyone.*
>   NOUN
>
> **b.** You need a noun for an object.
>
> INCORRECT: *Children need <u>loved</u>.*
>   VERB
>
> CORRECT: *Children need <u>love</u>.*
>   NOUN
>
> **c.** You need a noun for the object of a preposition. A noun always follows a preposition (*in, at, on, for, by, under, from,* etc.).
>
> INCORRECT: *She came to this country by <u>fly</u>.*
>   VERB
>
> CORRECT: *She came to this country by <u>airplane</u>.*
>   NOUN

2. Do I need a *singular or plural noun?*

> **a.** Do you need the plural form?
>
> INCORRECT: *She always carries many book.*
> CORRECT: *She always carries many books.* (*many* is a plural word)
>
> **b.** Do you need the singular form?
>
> INCORRECT: *The teacher gave a paper to every students.*
> CORRECT: *The teacher gave a paper to every student.* (*every* is a singular word)
>
> INCORRECT: *I hate homeworks!*
> CORRECT: *I hate homework!* (*homework* is a noncount noun. Noncount nouns are singular.)

3. Should I use an *adjective or an adverb?*

Adjective

a. Use an adjective before a noun.

He is a <u>healthy</u> <u>baby</u>.
       ADJ.   NOUN

b. Use an adjective after the verb *to be* and linking verbs (some linking verbs are: *to become, to seem, to look, to feel, to smell, to sound, to taste*).

It is <u>hot</u> today. (*is* is from the verb *to be*)
   ADJ.

You look <u>terrible</u>! (*look* is a linking verb)
        ADJ.

Adverb

a. When *look, feel, smell, sound,* and *taste* mean an action, they are followed by an adverb.

The thief looked <u>carefully</u> at the house. (*looked* is an action verb)
          ADVERB

b. Use an adverb to describe a verb.

The rabbit <u>jumped</u> <u>quickly</u> down its hole.
      VERB   ADVERB

c. Use *very* correctly.
  (1) with another adverb

  INCORRECT: *I very like to play golf.*

    CORRECT: *I like to play golf very much.*

  (2) with an adjective
  That tree is very old.

---

4. How do I *compare* things?

	Adjective	Comparative	Superlative
with one syllable	old big	older than bigger than	the oldest the biggest
with two syllables ending in *-y*	heavy noisy	heavier than noisier than	the heaviest the noisiest
with two or more syllables	beautiful expensive	more beautiful than more expensive than	the most beautiful the most expensive
irregular forms	good bad	better than worse than	the best the worst

Examples

1. *My father is* <u>*old*</u>.
2. *My sister is* <u>*older than*</u> *my brother.*
3. *My grandmother is* <u>*the oldest*</u> *person in our family.*

4. *Susan's car is* <u>*expensive*</u>.
5. *Mike's car is* <u>*more expensive than*</u> *Susan's car.*
6. *Ashley's car is* <u>*the most expensive*</u> *of all.*

7. *My handwriting is* <u>*bad*</u>.
8. *Phil's handwriting is* <u>*worse than*</u> *mine.*
9. *My doctor's handwriting is* <u>*the worst*</u> *in the world.*

1. Did I use the correct *preposition?*

PREPOSITIONS OF TIME		
in	I sleep late <u>in</u> the morning. She goes to class <u>in</u> the afternoon We eat dinner <u>in</u> the evening. My son was born <u>in</u> 1992. School begins <u>in</u> September.	in + the morning in + the afternoon in + the evening in + year in + month
at	Everyone sleeps <u>at</u> night. They play soccer <u>at</u> 4:00. I eat lunch <u>at</u> noon. He goes to bed <u>at</u> midnight.	at + night at + clock time at + noon at + midnight

on	I work <u>on</u> Saturday.
	 We were married <u>on</u> August 11th.
	 He calls her <u>on</u> Sunday night.
		on + day
		 on + date
		 on + day + morning
		                  afternoon
		                  evening
		                  night

from **from/to**	I will graduate four years <u>from</u> now. We study <u>from</u> 8 P.M. <u>to</u> 10:30.	from + a beginning time from + a beginning time to + an ending time
by	<u>By</u> 2050, people will live on the moon. (Meaning: Before January 1, 2050, people will live on the moon.)	by + a future time

A house stands **between** two trees. **In front of** the house, there are two children and a dog on the grass. The boy is **next to** the girl, and the dog is **beside** the girl. A car is **in** the driveway. A person is **under** the car, fixing it. A sailboat is **in** the river, and a bridge crosses **over** the river. A car is **in the middle of** the bridge. A truck is **behind** the car. Two birds are flying **above** the bridge, and, of course, the river is **below** the bridge. There are also several stores. A drugstore is **to the right of** a grocery store, and a furniture store stands **to the left of** the grocery store. There is a gas station **across from** the grocery store.

2. Did I use the *correct pronoun?*

Is the pronoun

  a. the **subject** of the sentence?

    He went to France.

  b. the **object** of the verb or of a preposition?

    Jason took her to the dance.

    Jason took Janet to it.

  c. used as an **adjective** to show **possession?**

    I washed my car.

  d. used as a **pronoun** to show **possession?**

    I washed mine.

Check the chart below to find out which pronoun you need.

Subject Pronoun	Object Pronoun	Possessive Adjective	Possessive Pronoun
I know Jim.	*Jim knows me.*	*That is my house.*	*That is mine.*
You know Jim.	*Jim knows you.*	*That is your house.*	*That is yours.*
He knows Jim.	*Jim knows him.*	*That is his house.*	*That is his.*
She knows Jim.	*Jim knows her.*	*That is her house.*	*That is hers.*
It knows Jim.	*Jim knows it.*	*That is its house.*	*That is its.*
We know Jim.	*Jim knows us.*	*That is our house.*	*That is ours.*
They know Jim.	*Jim knows them.*	*That is their house.*	*That is theirs.*

3. Should I use *to be* or *to have?*

Use *to be* with:	Use *to have* with:
a. adjectives *My father is short.* *Her sisters are studious.*	**a.** belongings *I have a new car.* *She has three brothers.*
b. nouns that describe the subject *I am a student.* *They are doctors.*	**b.** body parts *He has brown eyes.* *They have big feet.*
c. numbers for age and height. *She is 24 years old.* *He is over six feet tall.*	**c.** sicknesses *I have a cold.* *My mother has a weak heart.*

4. Should I use *scared, frightened,* or *afraid?*

	to scare	to frighten	afraid
verb (present)	*Horror movies scare me.*	*Horror movies frighten me.*	
verb (past)	*Last night, a movie on TV scared me.*	*Last night, a movie on TV frightened me.*	
adjective	*It was a scary movie.* *I was scared.*	*It was a frightening movie.* *I was frightened.*	*I was afraid.*

Note: 1. The past tense verbs *scared* and *frightened* have the same form as the adjectives *scared* and *frightened*
   2. There are two adjective forms, and they mean different things. In the first example, the word *"movie"* **gives** the scary or frightening feeling. In the second example, the word *"I"* **receives** the scared, frightened, or afraid feeling.

5. Should I use *fun* or *funny?*

a. *Fun* is a noun.
   I had fun at the beach last summer.
   I think water-skiing is a lot of fun.

b. *Funny* is an adjective.
   We all laughed at Bob's funny story.
   My uncle David is a very funny person.

Note: *Funny* is not the adjective form of *fun.* They have different meanings. Something "fun" gives us enjoyment. It is usually something that we like to do. Something "funny" makes us laugh.

1. Should I *add -s* or *-es* to verbs and nouns?

> **a.** For most words, add only *-s*. This is also the rule for words ending in *-e*.
> *run—runs*
> *dance—dances*
>
> **b.** If the word ends in *-s, -ss, -sh, -ch,* or *-x,* add *-es*.
> *bus—buses*
> *watch—watches*
> *kiss—kisses*
> *box—boxes*
> *brush—brushes*
>
> **c.** If the word ends in a vowel (a, e, i, o, u) **+ y,** add only *-s*.
> *toy—toys*
> *buy—buys*
>
> If the word ends in a consonant **+ y,** change the *-y* to *-i* and add *-es*.
> *study—studies*
> *fly—flies*

2. How do I *add -ed* and *-ing* to verbs?

> **a.** Verbs ending in *-e*
> • For *-ed* add only *-d*.
> *smile—smiled*
> *hope—hoped*
> • For *-ing* drop the *-e* and add *-ing*.
> *smile—smiling*
> *hope—hoping*
>
> **b.** Verbs ending in *-y*
> • For *-ed:*
> If there is a vowel (a, e, i, o, u) before the *-y,* keep the *-y*.
> *stay—stayed*
> *enjoy—enjoyed*
> If a consonant (all other letters) comes before the *-y,* change the *-y* to *-i*.
> *cry—cried*
> *hurry—hurried*

- For **-ing** add **-ing** to all verbs ending in **-y**.

  stay—staying
  cry—crying

c. Verbs ending in a consonant: Should I double the end consonant?

▌ ONE-SYLLABLE VERBS

If the verb ends in two consonants, add **-ed** or **-ing**.

  talk—talked—talking
   CC
  help—helped—helping
   CC

If the verb ends in a consonant and two vowels, add **-ed** or **-ing**.

  wait—waited—waiting
   VVC
  pour—poured—pouring
   VVC

If the verb ends in a consonant, a vowel, and another consonant, double the end consonant.

  hop—hopped—hopping
   CVC
  step—stepped—stepping
   CVC

*Exceptions: do not double **w** or **x**.

  snow—snowed—snowing
  mix—mixed—mixing

▌ TWO-SYLLABLE VERBS

If the verb ends in a consonant, a vowel, and another consonant, and if the accent
- is on the first syllable of the word, do not double the end consonant:

  listen—listened—listening
  offer—offered—offering

- is on the second syllable of the word, double the end consonant:

  permit—permitted—permitting
  prefer—preferred—preferring

3. Should I write *ie* or *ei*?

> This rhyme can help you remember whether to use *ie* or *ei*.
>
> > *I* before *E* except after *C*
> > or when sounded like *A*
> > as in *neighbor* or *weigh*
> >
> > *i* before *e*—*believe, niece, relief*
> > except after *c*—*receive, deceive, conceit*
> > or when sounded like *a*
> > as in *neighbor* or *weigh*—*eight, freight*
>
> *Exceptions: either, neither, height, foreign*

Punctuation

1. What punctuation do I need at the *end of a sentence?*

---

a. A statement ends with a period (.).
Today is Wednesday.

b. A question ends with a question mark (?).
Where are you going?

c. A sentence of strong feeling can end with an exclamation point (!).
I am very angry at you!

---

2. When do I need to use a *comma* (,)?

---

a. Use a commas in a list of more than two things.
She bought eggs, juice, milk, and bread at the store.

Do **not** use a comma in a list of only two things.

INCORRECT: *She bought eggs, and juice.*

CORRECT: *She bought eggs and juice.*

INCORRECT: *He laughed, and cried.*

CORRECT: *He laughed and cried.*

b. Use a comma in a compound sentence. Put a comma after the first independent clause.
It started to rain, so we hurried inside.

c. Use a comma in a complex sentence if the dependent clause comes before the independent clause.

While I was daydreaming, the teacher asked me a question.
    DEPENDENT CLAUSE   INDEPENDENT CLAUSE

Do **not** use a comma if the dependent clause comes after the independent clause.

The teacher asked me a question while I was daydreaming.
    INDEPENDENT CLAUSE   DEPENDENT CLAUSE

---

3. When do I need to use an *apostrophe (')?*

> **a.** Use an apostrophe to show possession (something belongs to someone).
>
> *I saw Ann's new car yesterday.* (The car belongs to Ann.)
>
> When the word ends in *-s,* add only an apostrophe.
>
> *I saw the boys' new bikes yesterday.* (The bikes belong to some boys.)
>
> **b.** Use an apostrophe when you make a contraction.
> *it's, there's, that's* (word + *is*)
> *can't, won't, wouldn't* (word + *not*)
> *she'll, I'll, that'll* (word + *will*)

4. How do I use *quotation marks (" ")?*

> When you tell a story, you often write words that people in the story say. When you do this, you must use quotation marks (" ") around those words. There are rules for using quotation marks. You must use them carefully!
>
> Look at these examples. Notice where the periods, commas, question marks, exclamation points, and quotation marks are placed.
>
> **a.** Speaker's name first:
> *Kelly said, "Open the door."*
>
> **b.** Speaker's name last:
> *"Open the door," said Kelly.*
>
> **c.** Speaker's name in the middle of a sentence:
> *"Open the door," said Kelly, "or I will knock it down!"*
>
> **d.** Speaker's name before or after two sentences:
> *Kelly said, "Open the door. If you don't, I will knock it down!"*
> *"Open the door. If you don't, I will knock it down!" said Kelly.*
>
> **e.** Speaker's name in the middle of two sentences:
> *"Open the door," said Kelly. "If you don't, I will knock it down!"*

C

Capitalization

1. What should I *capitalize?*

---

a. The first word in every sentence:
Her baby is beautiful.
The night was dark.

b. The pronoun *I*
My friend and I will wait here.
I think that I will stay home tonight.

c. Names:	*Susan Tuttle, Mark D. Wheaton*
d. Days:	*Sunday, Monday, Tuesday, etc.*
e. Months:	*January, February, March, etc.*
f. Holidays:	*Christmas, New Year's Day*
g. Nationalities:	*Egyptian, French, Thai*
h. Languages:	*Chinese, English, Arabic*
i. Cities:	*New York, Jakarta, Berlin*
j. Countries:	*Canada, Brazil, Australia*
k. Continents:	*South America, Africa, Europe*
l. Deity:	*God, Allah*

---

2. What should I *not capitalize?*

---

a. Seasons:	*spring, summer, winter, fall (autumn)*
b. Sports:	*basketball, tennis, football*
c. Subjects:	*mathematics, biology, history*
